PAM GREGORY discovered astrology (to Canada after university. Her passion years of intensive study at the Faculty of Astrological achieve Highest Honours in her Master's course. She now run a busy client practice in the New Forest, England. Her first book was the highly regarded *You Don't Really Believe in Astrology, Do You?*

Find out more at www.pamgregory.com.

Also by Pam Gregory

You Don't Really Believe in Astrology, Do You?

HOW TO CO-CREATE
using the
SECRET LANGUAGE OF THE UNIVERSE

PAM GREGORY

SilverWood

Published in 2017 by SilverWood Books

SilverWood Books Ltd
14 Small Street, Bristol, BS1 1DE, United Kingdom
www.silverwoodbooks.co.uk

ISBN 978-1-78132-684-8 (paperback)
ISBN 978-1-78132-685-5 (ebook)

British Library Cataloguing in Publication Data
A CIP catalogue record for this book is available from
the British Library

Page design and typesetting by SilverWood Books
Printed on responsibly sourced paper

HOW TO CO-CREATE USING THE
SECRET LANGUAGE OF THE UNIVERSE

Special thanks to my dear friend Nick, for his endless support, patience and help in the birthing of this book

Contents

	Notes to the Reader	11
1	The Journey	13
2	The Secret Language of the Universe	19
3	How Do We Create Our Reality?	27
4	Understanding your Unique Blueprint	41
5	Whispers of Your Future Self	57
6	Daily Context	109
7	Creating your Future Self	117
8	Lunations, Triggers in the Bigger Plan	141
9	Power Period 2017–2020	163
	Afterword	174
	Bibliography and Recommended Reading	175
	Organisations Teaching Astrology	177
	Endnotes	178

Notes to the Reader

"In the heavens you can see man, each part for itself; for man is made of heaven. And the matter out of which man was created also shows the pattern after which he was formed."

Paracelsus, from Paracelsian Medicine, in John Dee's Alchemical Diaries

This book has not been written to help you understand your entire birth-chart, as that is beyond the scope of one book: astrology is a vast subject. Neither will it be looking at the louder, more obvious parts of your chart; but it is focusing on the deepest, most mysterious and secret part of your birthchart that is the least well understood in Western astrology. If you like you can simply read the book straight through, but that would be missing a big opportunity in your self-understanding. It is intended to be a workbook for you to create your own alchemy, using your own birthchart downloaded free from my website using your date, time and place of birth, to help you answer the question: 'Why am I here?' You will be consciously co-creating as you work through this book, and understanding the best way to do that for your own life.

I hope you enjoy reading it as much as I have enjoyed writing it; I could not have imagined the deep soul journey on which it would take me. It has been a magic carpet ride.

1 The Journey

"If you wrote your memoir today, would your life be lived on the edge of possibility, if you held wonder in one hand and courage in another, and truly believed anything was possible?"

Jean Houston

Everyone is trying to get somewhere: a new job, a new home, a loving relationship, or trying to achieve a dream or vision. We are constantly in flux. Sometimes this can feel random and overwhelming. There are many books and self-help guides out in the world to help you, but for me there is always one vital missing step: they are general modalities; they are not specifically tailored to the individual with a deep understanding of who you are. True happiness goes beyond having a good job and a nice house. The most fundamental question in life for everyone is, 'who am I?'

The US Centre for Disease Control recently reported that 40% of Americans have not discovered a satisfying life purpose, and lack any sense of what makes their lives purposeful and meaningful. It is well known that having purpose and meaning in your life increases not only life satisfaction, but promotes mental and physical health. So if only we had some clear, reliable guidance from something or someone who had our best interests at heart, who wanted us to be the best that we could be at any moment as a unique individual, and that we could always rely on to give us insight and direction, wouldn't that be wonderful? Who wouldn't want to have that as a life tool?

This book is about that missing step, the appreciation of you as a unique individual, and how you can be empowered by that understanding. It will show you step by step how you can work practically with your own

13

birthchart, downloadable free from my website now (www.pamgregory.com), to co-create your reality more powerfully than you ever have before. This is the case even if you know nothing about astrology; this book will take you on an amazing journey of self-discovery.

By the end of reading this book you won't understand all of your birthchart, as that is a vast topic, but I'm going to be sharing some of the most profound elements of it so that you can start to live them in your own life from now on.

We are in times of seismic change in the world, and to help us navigate these changes you may have become familiar with the idea of 'co-creating your reality'. What does this really mean? How does it actually work? How can you start to apply some of those ideas in your own life to make a difference?

This book will look firstly at what we know about the nature of reality, and that perspective has changed dramatically over recent years. I will share this new information, as it forms a vital foundation for our 'missing step', the template determined at your birth from which you are *always* working, whether you know it or not. In the many thousands of charts I have studied over more than four decades, I have never known anyone who does not operate from their own template, their birthchart, their astrological DNA. No one's life is 'off strategy' relative to their birthchart. This is reflected in the many questions I will ask clients about dates in the past, specific experiences, and life-changing moments, all of which line up perfectly with their birthchart. It's the acorn which holds all the information for their life unfoldment. So we can't miss this step; we can't ignore our unique template.

Our birthchart is completely unique to us, determined by our time, date and place of birth. It is our individual life map, and gives us a practical framework to guide us, but it also operates at a profound soul level. Some describe it as 'a map of your soul on paper', for this birthchart represents, if you like, the picture on the front of the seed packet representing who you can fully become, your 'dharma'. I often describe this as your unique sheet of music, for it gives you your unique pattern, but it does not determine the *level* at which you play it. This is very important to understand. We can play it small or we can play it big, and the level of our consciousness determines that; but wherever we are at, our birthchart is an unparalleled guide to help us live our best life.

So the second part of this book is extremely practical, taking you step by step through how you can start to manifest powerfully by aligning with your very own unique birthchart. You will be focusing on a particularly deep part of your chart, and I'll be sharing some practical ways to start to live this. You can of course just read this book cover to cover, but you'll be missing a special opportunity in self-understanding, as the second part of this book is designed to be a workbook for you so that you can work through the process with your own chart, discovering your deeper purpose and soul's evolution as you get further into the chapters. I can't do this for you as I don't know your birthchart, so this is for you to discover. The more you put into this, the more you will get back in terms of who you are, and where you are meant to be focused in this life for your greatest growth.

This is a very exciting process, and anyone who has learned some astrology will have felt that frisson of excitement, knowing that it is the beginning of a fascinating journey of self-discovery. In my own life I still so clearly remember the afternoon I had my first astrological consultation over 40 years ago, and I can still feel that soaring exhilaration of seeing on paper in front of me that my life was not random, but is purposefully connected to the intelligence of the cosmos in a profound and mystical way. I have not stopped my study since that afternoon. There is still so much to know.

Don't worry if you have very little knowledge of astrology as you start to read this book. It will offer you rich understanding, whatever level of knowledge you have – even no knowledge. I often think of the analogy of skiing to astrology; whatever level you are at in skiing, whether you are just taking your first wobbly runs down the blue slopes, or happily rushing off-piste, you can get an enormous amount out of the experience. The same is true of astrology, so even if you are starting from zero knowledge, this book will help you live your life in a richer way.

Some people consider astrology to be a superficial irrelevance, as Sun sign astrology neatly divides the world's population into 12 equal sections and expects them to have a similar experience on any given day. That is the antithesis of serious astrology, where each person's birthchart contains up to 3,000 variables; serious astrology is multi-layered, multi-dimensional, like a hologram humming with information and meaning for each individual. We are going to be looking at some of the most important elements of your birthchart in this book.

Another reason that astrology is still broadly a 'missing step' in creating our lives is that even today it is a misunderstood language, lost in the mists of time from its origins in Ancient Mesopotamia 6,000 years ago. Also there is a secrecy about it, as for many centuries it has been highly esoteric, only studied in high academic and ecclesiastical circles by priests, astronomers and philosophers. Modern astrology has only existed for a very short time, effectively since the 1960s; and as it is still a profound mathematical and symbolic language that demands years of study to master fully, full of strange-looking symbols, it retains its air of mystery and obscurity. It is considered impenetrable by many. By the end of reading this book, you won't know all that astrology has to offer, but you will understand some of the deep and driving forces that make you who you are, and who you are meant to become in this life.

Astrology is the way that you can understand how you, as a unique individual, are connected to the divine intelligence which is always unfolding. We can track this in your birthchart at any moment. It is the hidden language which shows us how divine intelligence operates in the world, the invisible force that joins the quantum world with the world of matter and manifestation. In understanding this, we can co-create our reality in a powerful way.

It's a little like setting off to drive from London to Edinburgh, with no map and no idea how to get there, and we just try to guess our way there. Then someone gives us a map and a GPS, and that changes everything. We are then empowered to get to where we need to be, with clarity.

So this book will shed some light on astrology, but the purpose of it is to help you live a bigger, better life. How can you take this ancient, symbolic, mathematical language and make it operate in your life? How can you use it on a daily basis to enable you to discover and live who you really are, your authentic self? Your birthchart is the map that leads you back to your true self, and the closer your day-to-day life reflects who you really are, the better your life will work.

It wouldn't be possible to teach you all there is to know about astrology in just one book, but we are going to focus on your true 'soul destiny' which was set up for you at birth. This is one of the most profound aspects in your birthchart, and has taken me some years to understand. It forms the arrowhead of the 'future you', and the rest of your chart supports this development. How inspiring to have insight into this future you, that is your destiny, your reason for being on Earth? By reading this book, even with no astrological knowledge right now, you will be able to do that for yourself.

It will also explain how astrology is a vital, missing step in your empowerment. Remember that it will show you how you can use it *practically*, using your own birthchart from this point forward, to live a purposeful, fulfilling and joyful life. I wish you all blessings in that journey. My own life would have been so much less without this secret language of astrology to guide me.

2 The Secret Language of the Universe

"Man's relationship to the infinite began with the understanding that there was an orderliness to life, and this orderliness had its roots in the cosmos. Thus man discovered astrology as the study of his connection to the universe, and to a greater order."

Raymond Merriman, Astrologer

Since the beginning of recorded history, man has been observing the heavens. Astrology has ancient origins; animal bones from 25,000 years ago have been found near the source of the Nile which are cut with markings corresponding to the phases of the Moon; other records from 6,000 years ago in Ancient Mesopotamia, which is now modern-day Iraq, indicate that the planetary movements were closely observed. Throughout history, it has been considered a 'secret' language, although the reasons for that have changed over time. If you would like a much fuller version of the history of astrology, please refer to my first book, *You Don't Really Believe in Astrology, Do You?* The following historical summary helps us understand the obscurity of astrology through the ages.

Astrology originally developed from ancient peoples living open to the skies, observing the movements of the planets in the heavens, and correlating them with events on Earth. They started to notice patterns in how planetary aspects affected their agriculture, the best times for planting and harvesting. This continues today with biodynamic farming that is still practised widely in Europe. Understanding planetary patterns also gave a divine order to the rhythm of life; these ancient peoples believed that gods lived on the planets. They could see these planets with the naked eye, and they were keen to follow the 'instructions' from these gods to be in optimum flow with the universe. So from earliest times astrology was seen as a 'top-down' philosophy, that humankind was meant to observe and obey these planetary gods.

Astrology had a strong religious impetus in these very early times. It was a principal subject taught in the Mystery Schools which began almost 3,500 years ago, starting in Ancient Egypt and Babylon, with the sacred teachings spreading to the empires of India, Persia, Greece and Italy. The word 'mystery' comes from the Latin *'mysterium'*, meaning a secret rite or doctrine. The Mystery Schools were essentially religious schools where participation was reserved to initiates. There was much secrecy around these initiatory rituals, and as very strict oaths were taken before initiation, still very little is known of the details of Mystery Schools today. The purpose of the initiation was to place man in the cosmos as part of the divine order; this is something that continues in serious astrology today.

Despite the secrecy, it is known that the initiates had to study the motions of the planets, and be attuned to their energies before they could become priests or priestesses, and ceremonies took place at powerful times astrologically, such as Eclipses and solstices. Mathematics, medicine, astronomy, astrology, sacred geometry and ancient wisdom were taught in the Mystery Schools, and it was believed that both astronomy and astrology were vital subjects as they not only told the story of the past, present and future, but they helped the initiates get closer to the divine. Astrology in particular was considered to be divinely inspired. This strict secrecy helped to generate the myth that astrology was a magical subject.

The Mysteries were taught in the schools by priests, who were not as we imagine priests today; rather they were Astrologer-Priest-Hierophants, who possessed extraordinary knowledge. They had been initiated into all levels of the Mysteries themselves, which as well as study involved fasting and prayer. Part of the learning was that they saw death as simply the shift of the soul from one state of being, in one individual's body, to reappear in another. Therefore they believed that death affected the body, but not the soul. At the higher levels of initiation they believed the soul could be freed to commune with the divine; thus the purpose of their study was the rebirth of humans into higher consciousness. Astrology was a crucial part of this picture, as the Astrologer-Priest-Hierophants believed that the more you understood the planetary patterns, the more you were able to access divine intelligence. Therefore the priests produced a coherent philosophy that defined man's position in relation to the cosmos.

It is believed that these priests were not only aware of the astronomical cycle of the 'Great Year' of 26,000 years, otherwise known as the precession of the equinoxes, but they were also measuring it via the Giza plateau and its sphinx and pyramids that were used as a huge astronomical observatory. In addition these were considered to be places of mystical initiation.

The Greek philosophers Socrates, Plato and Pythagoras studied at the Mystery Schools, with Pythagoras (580–500 BCE) spending 22 years in the temples in Ancient Egypt as an initiate before opening his own school of philosophy in southern Italy. Plato and Pythagoras studied the secret doctrine of numbers, the heliocentric system of the universe (way before Galileo and Copernicus discovered this centuries later), astrology, astronomy and mathematics, all in the Mystery Schools. The knowledge and practices of these subjects were all held in secret, as the priesthood operated as a closed esoteric elite. Plato and Pythagoras became outstanding astrologers, mathematicians and philosophers, and have strongly influenced astrological thought, right down to the present day.

The knowledge was always protected by the priests, so never available to the common man, but used to the benefit of the kings, to help them manage their reign and war successes. The priests advised the monarch of the day on the affairs of state, and individual astrology did not appear until much later. The involvement of astrology with religion also continued up until the 17th century; it was taught in monasteries and ecclesiastical colleges through the Middle Ages up until the 1600s, and even the papacy had its own astrologer.

Astrology was considered 'higher knowledge', and therefore had become part of higher education through these centuries. If you were a university student, you would typically study mathematics, philosophy, theology and astrology. It was taught as part of the medical curriculum in universities across Europe, including Oxford and the Sorbonne. Galileo (1564–1642) taught it as part of the medical curriculum at the University of Padua, Italy.

Astronomy and astrology were also completely intertwined, with the brilliant minds of Plato, Pythagoras, Ptolemy, Hipparchus, Archimedes, Tycho Brahe, Johannes Kepler, Copernicus and Galileo all being immersed in both subjects as one. Mathematically, the measurement of astrology advanced under the Ancient Greeks, and during the Islamic Empire, with a school of astronomy and astrology being set up in Baghdad in 777 AD. Sadly, a huge amount of ancient astrological wisdom was lost in 640 AD when a large astrological library and school in Alexandria, Egypt, was set on fire by the armies of Caliph Omar. So this sense of obscurity about astrology, that any profound wisdom was solely the province of the educated and religious elite in society, continued through the centuries.

Medicine was another important strand that wove astrology into the fabric of society. Since earliest times, astrology was seen as a way of coming into harmony with the cosmos, and therefore returning the patient to good health. It was a question of balancing the four 'humours' within the patient, echoing the divine balance in nature. The Stoics, who lived around 250 BC, were scholars and philosophers, as well as physicians and astrologers, using astrology as a crucial part of their medical understanding. Astrology continued to be part of medicine through the centuries, and it was unthinkable even in the Middle Ages in Europe to become a doctor without a thorough understanding of astrology. Famous names such as Nicholas Culpeper (1616–1654), the herbalist and physician, and Robert Boyle (1627–1691), one of the founders of modern chemistry, used astrology widely in their practices.

So throughout history until the 17th century, astrology was seen as the province of the religious leaders, and the educated elite. This was reinforced during the Middle Ages as astrologers also held high positions in the royal courts in Europe, the papacy, and the Holy Roman Empire. They were a crucial part of every European monarch's decision-making team. Outstanding astrologers such as Brahe and Kepler were royal astrologers in the Holy Roman Empire, and Galileo held an important position with the high profile Medici family in Italy. One of the last great royal astrologers of these times was Dr John Dee (1527–1608), who held the favoured position to Elizabeth I of England. He was a brilliant scholar, academic, mathematician, navigator, astronomer and astrologer, and a fellow of St John's College, Cambridge. Elizabeth I even used him as an ambassador for England on several occasions.

Dr John Dee followed in the tradition of Plato and Pythagoras, believing that mathematics underpinned the universe. He was an alchemist, constantly trying to turn metals into different forms; but alchemy was actually much broader than this, encompassing philosophy, Hermeticism, sacred geometry, chemistry and astrology. Dee believed that man had the potential for divine power, following in the teachings of the Mystery Schools. Alchemy was not just about making gold, it was about transmuting the baser elements of the human character to release the divine within the individual. It was the investigation of how the material and matter of life could be transformed into the spiritual. John Dee's explorations into this had a sense of mission: alchemy was greater than chemistry; it was the way to release man's divine power, to enable him to reach enlightenment.

Dee's immersion in the Hermetic tradition of 'as above, so below', led him to believe that astrology was not only a universal law of creation but that it was in fact the *secret language of the universe,* and he was determined to find a way to prove that using alchemy. He felt that as each of the planets' symbolism is linked to a physical substance, for instance metals such as gold for the Sun, silver for the Moon, and lead for Saturn, he would find some clues in the actual physical structure of the universe to help explain further this 'secret language'. He had a laboratory in London where these strange experiments took place, and where he also practised his astrology.

Dee introduced a greater level of mysticism into astrology, as he began to converse with angels, and his writings on this were prolific. He wrote *John Dee's Five Books of Mystery,* which detailed his advanced studies in Enochian magic with angels. These Five Books of Mystery were discovered long after his death in a hidden compartment of an old chest with some other magical writings, although he had 'promised the angels' that he would not reveal his writings to anyone. They contain many mystical truths that scholars are continuing to investigate, and became a focus of study of the Hermetic Order of the Golden Dawn.

The Hermetic philosophy of 'as above, so below' principle means that our reality on Earth is merely a reflection of the cosmos; the microcosm reflects the macrocosm. This is an underlying principle that I work with every day as an astrologer, for I am translating the symbolism and geometry of the astrological patterns to have meaning in the lives of individuals.

This Hermetic philosophy believes that the movements of the planets hold meaning beyond the laws of physics, as symbols in the mind of divine consciousness, or God. This was a crucial underpinning of their teaching, which included the esoteric subjects of the Qabalah, alchemy, sacred geometry, and astrology. These were all considered disciplines by which you could get closer to the divine. This also echoed both the Ancient Greeks' and the Mystery Schools' understanding of astrology.

The Mystery Schools' traditions continued in the form of Rosicrucianism, which began in the early 17th century. This secret society was based on esoteric truths from the ancient past, which *"concealed from the average man, provide insight into nature, the physical universe, and the spiritual realm"* (my italics). The teachings included Hermetic philosophy, astronomy, astrology, sacred geometry and philosophy. Anonymous Rosicrucian manifestos were published in Europe between 1607 and 1616 that declared the existence of a 'secret brotherhood of alchemists and sages', who were preparing to change the cultural, political and religious life of Europe. Like the Mystery Schools, initiates had to go through secret rituals, and the Rosicrucian Society was often referred to as the 'College of Invisibles'. They published no specific locations, but believed that 'the real desire of the seeker will lead us to him and him to us.'

The fact that astrology and astronomy played an important part in this secret society was supported by the involvement of great astronomer/astrologers such as Johannes Kepler, Tycho Brahe and Dr John Dee.

So the important theme here is that serious astrology was not understood by the ordinary people; it was a scholarly, scientific, mathematical, religious and even mystical philosophy, studied and used by the educated in society, in secret societies, and those who held high positions. It was deliberately kept hidden by those with knowledge of it, such as the priests who were obliged to take oaths to maintain its secrecy, as it was seen as very powerful. Historically its use was almost entirely 'mundane', concerning the affairs of state, agriculture, wars, and the fate of kings. The average person in the street would not have been able to study and understand it. All of this reinforced the sense of obscurity around astrology, and as a result it held high status, and was much respected.

The way that astrology was viewed began to change during the 1600s, with the arrival of René Descartes (1596–1650) and Isaac Newton (1643–1726), and their mechanistic philosophies of how the universe worked. These laid the foundation for the so-called Age of Enlightenment. Newton's Laws of Motion were seen to define the known universe at the time. He was aware of astrology, but based on his new theories he clearly stated that the planets were too far away to have any influence based on gravity, and that astrology was poor thinking and 'superstition'; it was dismissed to the periphery of society, and lost all academic respectability. In this new age of scientific enquiry, it could not be proved to work on mechanical principles. It was a big fall from its previously highly esteemed position in society, when it had been interwoven with medicine, mathematics, astronomy, religion, theology, university education, and royal positions.

From the mid-1600s to 1900, astrology went through a 'dry period', when there was little intellectual development of the subject. As a result of Newton's Laws and views, intellectual classes moved away from astrology, fearing that Newton might be right. Astrological almanacs over this period were popular, but they were largely predicting peace or war, or the fate of the king. They were used for political propaganda, or gave predictions for the weather with regard to agriculture. The astrology of the almanacs was a very long way from anything we would consider psychological astrology today, and the subject fell from intellectual life dramatically. The educated classes did not want to be judged as 'unscientific' in light of Newton's exciting new Laws of Motion. So for instance, Raphael's Predictive Almanacs from the 1850s would have predictions such as 'a child born on this day will suffer many ills'; they were highly fatalistic and unrealistic. So whether it was a 'secret language' because it was the province of the elite in society, or as during these fallow 250 years, the driving force had gone from the subject with few intellectuals interested in pursuing it, its obscurity remained.

From around 1900 to 1940 astrology began to be revived with the Theosophists, the eccentric and mystical Madame Blavatsky, and the work of Rudolf Steiner. In part they were following the Mystery School teachings, and developing them further. Around the same time, the philosophers Krishnamurti and Ouspensky also begin to revive astrology as a sacred science. Carl Gustav Jung (1875–1961) used astrology to help diagnose his patients, and as inspiration for his psychological theories of synchronicity and archetypes, but aside from that the Second World War had put a halt to any further astrological development. So it is incredibly recently that modern-day astrology as we know it today began to be birthed out of this background, and the more psychological understanding of astrology began from around the 1960s. It is important to say, however, that for the vast majority of its 6,000-year history, people have regarded this as a language of fate. Planets 'do things to you'; you are a tiny recipient of these huge cosmic forces.

Astrology forecasts started to appear in newspaper columns in England in the 1930s, and in this way it popularised Sun sign astrology that continues today. Sun sign astrology is embarrassingly trivial and again, fatalistic, as it is depicted in these columns. Sadly the common understanding of astrology today is still that of Sun signs (if it were that easy it wouldn't have taken me more than 40+ years of practice), as that is the way that people generally come in contact with astrology day to day, and the prevailing attitude is still that we are victims of our astrological fate. Even today the messages I receive from prospective clients illustrate this attitude: that we are victims of the planets. Even for those people who have some astrological knowledge, it is common for them still to see their birthcharts in a 'Newtonian' way: that life's events happen to you from the outside in, and then you have to react to them.

However, this book is going to turn all of that thinking on its head. All of us, whether we realise it or not, live from the inside out; we are constantly living out our birthchart, even if we are playing our music badly. I can say this with conviction, having studied thousands of birthcharts, and seeing how everyone's lives are reflecting their birthchart, this map of their soul, at every moment. This book is going to show you how astrology is a language of empowerment; that we are not victims of our fate, but heroes of our lives. It is about practically co-creating your own life, every day, maximising your potential and living a life full of purpose and meaning. You will be living out your 'dharma', the destiny you came here to fulfil. Astrology is a language of our spiritual evolution, and the better we understand it, the more easily we can become who we are meant to become.

In a sense, this book is echoing some of the Mystery School teachings: that the soul has its own journey within but also beyond this life, and that astrology can help to guide us and raise our consciousness in this evolution of the soul. It can help us to co-create more effectively, once we understand that it is a language of interconnectedness. Every birthchart is not only a picture of the heavens at the moment of birth, but also a map of the psyche and potential life journey for that individual. It is inner and outer at the same time. It is a pivot point of creation. The better we understand this profundity, the more we can see that how we use our unique astrological pattern will produce a mirror of our inner reality out in the world. That is my daily bread and butter as an astrologer.

Firstly, let's consider some of the quantum understanding of how reality is created.

3 How Do We Create Our Reality?

"Quantum science suggests the possibility of many possible futures for each moment in our lives. Each future lies in a state of rest until it is awakened by choices made in the present."

Gregg Braden

Many of us have heard of the theory of co-creation – that we are responsible for co-creating our reality – but I suspect few of us live that way all the time. Most of us still operate in the all-pervasive old Newtonian paradigm of living in a random way, hoping that someday the right job, partner, or house will show up for us. We may wait a lifetime for this to happen. This is a very disempowered way to live, as it is living from the outside in. We *are* then living in 'victim' mode, subject to the whims of those people and events we come into contact with. However, there is an enormous amount of evidence now in the area of quantum physics, as well as in my own study of thousands of birthcharts, that we live from the inside out, not the outside in. That's what your birthchart is all about; it is the acorn that contains all the information for you to turn into you, and blossom into your dharma, that which you are meant to become. It is the music you are playing out in the world.

In addition, we live in the illusion that the universe is already complete, and we are in some way separate from it, and therefore we're being imposed upon it. This is not the case, as the universe is never complete, and you and I are constantly contributing to its manifestation, creation and evolution, whether we recognise it or not. Fortunately, we have a lot of evidence now as to how we do this, even if we may be unaware of it.

You may have learned at school via models with big polystyrene balls linked together that molecules were made up of atoms and electrons, which were solid, as the diagrams suggested. We think that the world is made up of solid things. However, the more we understand quantum theory, this teaches us that even if things appear to be solid, we, and they, are simply vibrating energy. As human beings, we are made up of 0.0001% matter; all the rest is energy.

That means that if you were to fly through your cells and atoms with a camera, taking photos all the time, there would be almost nothing on the film at the end. We have an illusion of solidity, but everything is energy. We know from quantum theory that everything exists merely as an infinite sea of possibilities, as pure energy. Electrons are not solid matter, and only change from a wave of possibility into a particle of matter when they are observed, when attention is given to them. They then collapse from a wave of nothingness into an event or experience. This is known as the 'observer effect'. In fact Niels Bohr, one of the founders of quantum theory, said, "Everything we call real is made up of things that cannot be regarded as real." It is only the interaction of our consciousness, whether we are aware of it or not, that produces solid reality in the form of an event or experience. As B. Alan Wallace, lecturer, scholar writer on Tibetan Buddhism said: "Let's assume the whole universe is a quantum system…when you take out the observer-participant, you have a problem of frozen time; the universe does not evolve, it doesn't change, nothing happens."

Indeed, it is this very act of observation that *creates* matter. The universe is interactive. So each of us has a vital, active, participatory role to play in creating our reality and our lives in total. This 'observer effect', well known in science, clearly demonstrates our interaction with the universe. There is a constant interplay, every second, between us and it, a constant energetic communication. Our consciousness is linked to the wider cosmos, and astrology gives us the evidence of this at every moment, but we don't see this from our everyday state of being.

This is incredibly empowering, as we move from victim to participant and co-creator in a very real way. This observer effect must also mean that we have access to a *higher level of causation* that can turn these possibilities into material reality. It is very hard work to create from 3D reality, trying to force things to go your way. It is so much easier to achieve from a slightly altered state, which we will be describing later in this book, and create from a higher state of being; we are then effecting 'downward causation' to produce our reality.

The power of our consciousness is far greater than we might imagine.

Indeed, consciousness is the creator of the manifest universe, as it constantly creates matter. It is by observation, or by focusing our attention, that we create. Of course if we are unaware of this we are still creating all the time, but by default, from a less conscious and probably less positive frequency than our potential can offer. So our reality is not set or fixed; it is pliable, and we can change how it manifests by shifting our emotional state and focus. As Werner Heisenberg, one of the founders of quantum theory, states: "The atoms or elementary particles themselves are not real; they form a world of potentialities or possibilities rather than one of things or facts."

We have an enormous amount of evidence now that consciousness affects matter. We have the impressive work of Masaru Emoto, who studied water crystals. He conducted extensive studies where he asked people to direct specific emotions to water samples, and the emotions included love, hate, joy, gratitude, envy, and many more. The water samples were then frozen, and dramatically different shapes appeared in the crystals. Those that had hate or any negative emotion directed at them were ugly and twisted, with no coherence in their shape. However those that had received positive emotions such as love or gratitude had formed exquisitely beautiful symmetry in the crystals. His work demonstrates the power of our emotions by making them visual. When you consider that each of us is around 90% water, it is not a big jump to understand how our own emotions affect our bodies. We also know from the Nobel-prize winning work of Candace Pert, author of *Molecules of Emotion*, that each change of emotion we experience through our days results in a cascade of changes in our neuropeptides, changing the biochemistry of every cell in our bodies. Our bodies are merely a printout of our consciousness. This is a direct consciousness-physical matter connection.

Dr Joe Dispenza, neuroscientist, is conducting ongoing studies into the brain, and has measured the brainwaves of several thousands of his students at workshops around the world. He does this as they begin and sustain meditation. The shift of consciousness on entering a meditative state produces dramatically different brainwaves in seconds. Our shift of consciousness changes our energy, physically. An even simpler example is blushing; if we are embarrassed, in a second our face flushes and betrays our feelings. So consciousness has a direct effect at the physical level, and is measurable.

If you take a roller coaster ride and are terrified, you will dramatically increase the amount of the stress hormone, cortisol, in your blood. However, if you see this same ride as an exhilarating and exciting experience, you will produce chemicals such as interferon, a powerful cancer-killing agent. Your body is a pharmacy that responds to the emotion you are feeling, rather than the objective fact. It is translating how you *feel* about the experience. This is a very physical expression, as your biochemistry in every cell of your body, at any moment, is responding to your thoughts, emotions, and your consciousness. This shows us that it is not the event itself that is the determinant of the body's chemistry, but how we react to events emotionally that does that.

However, our thoughts and emotions not only directly affect our own bodies, they affect other people too. We are not as separate as we think.

Let's look a little more closely at what we know about this.

It was Fritz-Albert Popp, a German biophysicist, who originally discovered that our DNA constantly emits light, via tiny microtubules in each of our cells, in the form of biophotons. Some people can actually see this energetic 'glow' around people's heads and bodies, which is the radiance of this light. So as living beings all of us are sending out these tiny currents of light constantly. Light carries information, and so the thoughts we are thinking are being broadcast out to the world all the time. A magnetoencephalograph, where the probes don't even touch the head, can measure our electromagnetic field, as proof that we are broadcasting our thoughts and energy all of the time. This electromagnetic field is produced by the electrical impulses of our thoughts within our brains. Others can pick up on our thoughts, again as evidence that they are not contained within our skulls, but constantly being sent out to the world. I have personally been involved in many experiments where I have to understand the thoughts of others via a phone line from the other side of the world, when the only piece of information I have about them is their first name. It is remarkable how often, and how easily, we are able to do this without any training. We catch each other's energy like we catch a cold, and we catch their thoughts too.

Looking at this in more detail, biophotons are actually used in the cells of living organisms to communicate, as this energy/information system via light is dramatically faster than any chemical exchange in the body. Fascinatingly, biophoton emissions also change through our Sun/Earth day; they are consistently lower in the morning than in the afternoon. Science is now recognising the ability of the human body to not only emit energy via biophotons, but also to receive energy and information from the Sun;

it's like our skin cells are all tiny solar panels. So our bodies' biophoton outputs are governed by solar and lunar forces, as their rhythm of output changes through the day. Again, this demonstrates that there is very precise interaction between living beings at the cellular level, and the movements of the Earth around the Sun on a daily basis. That's how interconnected we are.

The respected HeartMath Institute in America is measuring how our individual magnetic fields are interacting with the Earth's magnetic field from various monitors around the world as part of the Global Coherence Initiative, as they "believe there is a feedback loop between human beings and the Earth's energetic/magnetic systems." They state "it is well established that the resonant frequencies in the Earth's various magnetic fields directly overlap with those of the human brain, cardiovascular and autonomic nervous systems[1]." The scientific community is beginning to appreciate and understand at the deeper level how we are all interconnected with and affected by the magnetic fields generated by the Sun and the Earth: "every cell in our bodies is bathed in an external and internal environment of fluctuating invisible magnetic forces. Human psychological rhythms and behaviours are synchronised with solar and geomagnetic activity, so fluctuations in the Earth's and Sun's magnetic fields can affect virtually every circuit in human as well as biological systems[2]." Don't forget that the brain and heart are sensitive electromagnetic organs, so these statements are perhaps not surprising.

The connection of our own magnetic field to that of the Earth is very specific. The Earth has a natural pulse of 7.83Hz, known as the Schumann resonance. This is exactly the frequency of human alpha waves where we feel a sense of well-being, relaxation, and creativity. It boosts our immune system. An experiment conducted by Professor Wever from the Max Planck Institute in the 1960s demonstrates the power and importance of this physical link with the Earth. He took a group of volunteers, and for four weeks they lived in a bunker which completely screened out the Earth's natural resonance. Professor Wever noticed that their health progressively deteriorated. Their circadian rhythm, the day-night cycle, became disrupted. They suffered sleep deprivation, migraine headaches, and emotional distress. The deterioration was physical, mental and emotional. Without the volunteers being aware, Professor Wever introduced a natural pulse of 7.83Hz into the volunteers' living accommodation, and the body measurements which were being constantly monitored rapidly improved. We are naturally hard-wired to the Earth's heartbeat.

Recently the Schumann resonance has been spiking up as high as 45Hz as measured by the HeartMath monitors, and the HeartMath Institute believe that the more we are coming together as a heart-based community, expressing love, gratitude or appreciation, high level emotions of coherence, the more we can create spikes in the Earth's field. Changes in consciousness as a result of global peace meditations, expressing heart-based emotions, are reflected in the measurements of the Earth's field. So all of us are inextricably linked, via our own individual magnetic fields, to that of the Earth. We are constantly interacting with the Earth's field; we are broadcasting our thoughts and emotions into the field, and equally we are receiving information back from it. The ancient peoples as far back as the rishis of India spoke of our connection to the Earth's heartbeat. Now we have scientific evidence.

This may also give us definite proof of the link between our thoughts, emotions and intentions with the Earth's field that we may previously have thought of as insubstantial and not very important. It starts to give much more weight to our thoughts and emotions, and we start to have an 'energetic' understanding of how intention may work. This hypothesis also means that we are all interconnected, and it is our individual and collective energy that can make a difference in the world. We will start to have a much greater sense of the power of this over the next few years, that we are literally individual and collective co-creators of our destiny.

In fact, our energetic relationship with the Earth and the cosmos may be much more complex and intertwined than we had ever imagined. The HeartMath Institute have discovered that even trees have a circadian, or day-night rhythm, and these electrical rhythms are tied into the gravitational pull of the Earth. The daily rise and fall of human biochemical markers (uric acid levels, blood pressure, hormones and many more) are connected to this Sun/Moon/Earth relationship. Franz Halberg, a scientist deeply involved in 'chronobiology', states that all living things are connected to the Earth's 24-hour rotation. So it isn't only the biomarkers of we humans, but also those of single-celled organisms from millions of years ago that are synchronised by the planets and the Sun. Although the Sun sustains life, in that it provides heat and light, it has a much bigger role in our 24-hour biochemistry. As Lynne McTaggart says: "The Sun is a giant metronome, setting the pace for all life.[3]"

However, what is fascinating is if we go beyond physical survival to thinking about setting intentions to effect change, it appears more than our relationship with the Sun is involved. Michael Persinger, cognitive neuroscience researcher, university professor and long-time investigator of ESP, telepathy, and various psychic experiments, says that the best time for the greatest success in these endeavours is "around 1pm local *sidereal time,* which is time measured by our relation to the *stars, not the Sun*[4]" (italics mine). This certainly hints at a much deeper relationship with the cosmos than we may ever have imagined, even going beyond our own Sun, and the capacity we have to use cosmic patterns to maximise our results. One of the reasons astrology is so powerful is that it is using the understanding of planetary patterns to maximise our potential at any given moment.

Dean Radin, Chief Scientist at the Institute of Noetic Sciences, has been involved in collecting data from random number generators (RNGs) sited at 70 venues across the world. When synchronisation of emotion occurs at big emotional events, such as 9/11, it produces changes in the output of the random number generators, which are one in a million odds against the effect being due to chance. Just before the attacks on the World Trade Center began, the output of the random number generators started to become more coherent, as the world's attention, all experiencing similar emotions, was focused on this event. This continued through the time of the attacks, and a little afterwards. So the peak in emotion created a peak in coherence in the RNGs, as the world's attention was concentrated on this. The emotion changed the randomness of the RNGs' output. The same effect was seen at the death of Princess Diana, another highly emotional event for much of the world. This is demonstrating a direct link between human emotion and a physical effect.

Dean Radin has also been involved in hundreds of meditation studies, when RNGs were watched while meditation was taking place with a large group. Sometimes the meditators were aware of the study, sometimes not. Either way, the RNGs showed increased coherence during the period of meditation. Therefore Dean Radin's work seems to show that coherent consciousness creates order in the world[5]. This is very powerful as a conclusion, as it dramatically changes the Newtonian materialistic world view, and demonstrates our ability as co-creators.

Hundreds of studies have been done on the effect of directed consciousness to affect change in the world. For example, one study was done during the Israel-Lebanon war in the 1980s. Two Harvard professors organised groups of experienced meditators in Jerusalem, Yugoslavia and the US with the purpose of focusing attention on an area of conflict at various intervals over a 27-month period. During the study, the levels of violence in Lebanon decreased between 40–80% each time a group was meditating. The average number of people killed in the war each day fell from 12 to 3, and the war-related injuries fell by 70%[6].

A carefully controlled study was conducted in Washington DC to reduce crime levels in 1993 which involved 4,000 meditators from 81 countries, focused on reducing crime rates in the Washington area. The success of the eight-week study exceeded expectations: the findings showed that the rate of violent crime decreased by 23.6% during the June 7 to July 30 experimental period. The odds of this result occurring by chance are less than two in one billion[7].

Entire books have been written on the powerful effect of consciousness on matter and events, even at a distance. The effect is non-local, so geography becomes irrelevant, as the quantum field operates on a non-local basis. Lynne McTaggart's *The Intention Experiment* is a brilliant book sharing examples of intention, including many of her own powerful studies, which are ongoing. I have personally participated in several of them, and seen the evidence with my own eyes. As Lynne says: "a thought is not only a thing; it is a thing that influences other things."

Intention is defined as a 'directed thought to perform a determined action'. It has a sense of focus, momentum and propulsion, as opposed to our daily scattered thoughts. Biophotons that are regulated by the Sun/Earth relationship that we discussed above play a crucial role in intention. Quoting from a recent commentary in the journal *Investigacion Clinica*, "The emission of light particles (biophotons) seems to be the mechanism through which an intention produces its effects. Direct intention manifests itself as an electrical and magnetic energy producing an ordered flux of photons. Our intentions seem to operate as highly coherent frequencies capable of changing the molecular structure of matter.[8]"

So here we have it again: we set intention, our directed thought, and this is communicated to the universe by biophotons, which we emit but also receive in energy from the Sun; and this intention can change the structure of matter. Thoughts are looking less wafty by the moment. Remember the scientific basis for this is light, and when we get further into this book, you will be setting your own intentions for your own future, and using this practically. Imagine then that you are sending out a stream of coherent light to the universe in order to manifest your wishes, for that, apparently, is exactly what you are doing.

So we are not separate from the universe, we are inextricably linked participants of it, constantly influencing the Earth's field and our own reality. We are in a constant feedback loop of sending out our energy via our magnetic field to that of the Earth, and receiving information back from it. This becomes incredibly empowering, as every single one of us matters in the ongoing evolution of the Earth's field. It is via this field that we are all interconnected.

Therefore not only are our bodies, lives and consciousness connected to this pliable jelly-that-has-not-yet-set reality, but we are a *flowing extension* of it. David Bohm, Professor of Theoretical Physics at London University, felt that energy was merely a sliding scale between each of us and our outer reality. Remember that we are not solid; only 0.0001% of each of us represents solid matter – the rest is energy. Fred Alan Wolf, physicist, echoing the same thought, says that: "no clear dividing line exists between ourselves and the reality we observe to exist outside of ourselves[9]". This fluidity gives us the empowering opportunity, constantly, to affect what manifests in our lives. Try thinking of yourself and your outer reality as less solid, dense and tangible, but more holographic in nature; as spheres of shimmering, vibrating energy, all in a state of constant flux.

Indeed, quantum physicists have discovered that physical atoms are made up of vortices of energy that are constantly spinning and vibrating. This means that matter at its tiniest observable level is energy, and we know that our consciousness is connected to it. Energy can exist as a wave, or a particle. A particle is clearly denser, having condensed into matter. In ordinary, everyday states as we go about our daily lives, the mind is more particle-like, and tends to be located in time and space with a clear sense of who we are as an identity, and therefore often a sense of separateness. However, once we can access higher states of emotion and being (such as joy, love, gratitude, appreciation), our minds become more 'wavelike', and no longer fixed in time and space; we can then start to create more easily from this heightened state. In fact what happens is that we are accessing the quantum field more frequently within every second, and our increased interaction with this field of probability gives us more influence over it, in terms of pulling our desired manifestation from the quantum soup. Reinforcing this idea of a non-set reality, to quote Werner Heisenberg: "atoms are not things, they are only *tendencies*" (italics mine). Each of us can have an effect on the way these 'tendencies' fall.

One very powerful step for each of us in the creation of our reality is the unique 'template' which we each operate from, and that is your birthchart. Consider this to be like your DNA; you can only create cells from this blueprint, and equally it seems that your experiences will always reflect your birthchart. *We can't miss this intervening step*, and it gives us so much more understanding of our individual process.

After studying many thousands of charts, it is clear that people's lives always are 'on strategy' with the unfolding symbolism in their charts. A life is never 'off strategy'. We may play our unique sheet of music badly or beautifully, but that is the sheet of music that will play in our lives. Therefore when we are thinking about creating our reality, it is not so much of a leap from us as an individual, to an amorphous, apparently infinite, yet-to-be-determined reality. We have to use our unique template, consciously or unconsciously, that will offer us different opportunities in different areas of life over time. Our blueprint isn't optional.

At certain times, your career may be emphasised. At other times, it may be your relationships, or your health. We have to go via our template, as our lives will always fall in line with our individual astrological pattern that is naturally unfolding, and that is different for everyone at any moment. Whether we are playing it harmoniously or discordantly, our birthchart is the music we are playing. We have no choice in the birthchart we are operating from – at least once we have arrived on Earth – but we have a big choice in the *way* we play our music. We can play it with an old spoon on a rusty box, or we can play it magnificently with all the elements of the orchestra. This is where our free will comes in. Your birthchart determines your unique *pattern*, it does not determine the *level* at which you will live it. Your consciousness does that.

Our level of consciousness is affected by the way we react to life's events. When something significant happens in our lives, let's say we suddenly lose our job, we have a 'choice point'. This is where our freewill makes a decision how to react to this situation. We can say, "Oh these things always happen to me, I'm such a loser, I'll never find the right job." That reaction will tend to induce a frequency of misery, depression and pessimism, and therefore we will be tuned to 'Radio Misery' when co-creating the next stage in our lives, and events on the same frequency will be attracted towards us, as we are beings of vibrational frequency. However, if we react by saying to ourselves, 'Actually, that job wasn't right, and I know it; now I can find the job that will really make me feel fulfilled and valuable,' we are now tuned vibrationally to 'Radio Optimism', and are much more likely to attract a positive event into our lives.

As Carl Jung said, it is not what happens to us in life, it is how we react to what happens to us that determines character; and I might add, destiny. Your emotional set point affects your level of consciousness, particularly at 'choice point' moments like this, and therefore the level from which you will be co-creating the next episode. Thoughts and emotions are the bridge between our inner and outer worlds. If you believe you are a loser, the world will probably treat you like one. Your outer reality is a mirror for your internal state. So it is super important to take a moment to catch yourself in any instinctive reaction, to optimise your frequency. We will be looking at the practicalities of this in a later chapter.

However, once we start to understand our birthchart, we have a huge advantage in creating our reality. We can start to live strategically. We can understand where and when specific opportunities are coming up for us, whether it is in career, finance, personal growth, or any area of life. We can then focus our frequency, consciousness and attention on those areas, knowing that we have the universe at our back. We are flowing with what naturally wants to unfold, rather than fighting the current. Things will manifest much more easily then, as we are helping the acorn to become an oak tree, not a chrysanthemum.

Astrology is a language of mathematical probability. In any birthchart I am always looking for a convergence of aspects to produce an event. For instance, recently a client was very keen to know the most likely time for her to become pregnant, as she was now 40. She already had one young child. So in the analysis, I was not only looking for a convergence of aspects in her own birthchart that suggested joy at the pregnancy (5th house of the birthchart, which rules children) followed by motherhood some months later (5th house, but also 10th house of status), I was looking for a convergence of aspects in her husband's chart of a new child (5th house) and joy with his wife (7th house, marriage partner), and in her young son's chart I was looking for a new sibling arriving (3rd house, siblings). Then the mathematical probabilities across all three birthcharts converged into a specific time period, which was the best time for her to pursue IVF with a new baby appearing nine months later. The joy of the pregnancy had to obviously link up in time with the birth of a new baby a few months later. Beautifully, these timings all manifested in the birth of a baby girl, exactly as had been anticipated in the timing.

This is an incredibly important point: **just like the quantum universe, the level at which your destiny manifests is not yet fixed. It lies in the realm of 'probability'. Both quantum reality and astrological reality deal with 'probable' outcomes, not set**. I recommend that you read that sentence again, as it has profound implications. However, knowing how your music is most likely to unfold enables you to focus on the best, highest probable outcome you could wish for, and then you are then focusing your attention and consciousness on manifesting that. The pattern in your birthchart, your template, together with the frequency of your consciousness, will draw events to you in line with that vibration. You are then using the probability of the quantum, together with the probability of your astrological destiny, to produce what you want. *In fact, they become one and the same thing.* You can only manifest what is in your birthchart at any moment, and therefore the quantum field and your birthchart pattern operate as one, with you pulling your desired manifestation to you, at a time when this was already due to unfold in your life. You are focusing on your optimum manifestation in line with the divine organising intelligence of the cosmos.

As Tom Campbell, a physicist who previously worked at NASA, stated recently: "Matter at the micro and macro levels is simply (the result of) probability distributions,[10]" meaning a focus of energy that condenses to form matter.

What reinforces this idea of quantum probability being the same as your astrological probability is that any birthchart is a map of the heavens at the moment of your birth, and also a map of your psyche and your future unfolding. It is inner and outer at the same time; a reflection of the planetary patterns way out in space, and equally your inner landscape, representing your reason for being here on Earth. It therefore on paper represents the pivot point between your life potential and manifestation. This intersection of quantum probability with your individual birthchart is so powerful, and it feels sacred every time I hold a consultation. We can change the level at which our future operates by consciously raising our energy, and focusing on our desired outcome ready to unfold in our birthchart. We can use the understanding of our birthchart as the springboard for a higher level of manifestation in our lives.

I believe your birthchart operates at this high level of the implicate, not yet manifested, and that you are offered this in life as your manifesting template, your life plan blueprint. This becomes an empowered and incredibly exciting way to live, as your journey becomes very conscious. You start to feel yourself in the magic zone. Manifestation becomes so much easier when you understand the sheet of music you are playing.

We are going to look into how we use this information very practically in a later chapter, particularly the understanding of 'convergence', maximising the probability. This is a very important concept. The knowledge that your birthchart actually describes your quantum probability at any time came to me in a dream, and had a profound effect on me. In essence, *your birthchart gives you the language of the cosmos, and of your powerful co-creating potential within it*. This is the secret language of the universe, postulated over 400 years ago by Dr John Dee.

4 Understanding your Unique Blueprint

"If all the information of the cosmos flows through our pores at every moment, then our current notion of our human potential is only a glimmer of what it should be."

Lynne McTaggart

Everyone's chart is completely unique, and will never be repeated in history again. That is an amazing thought, and shows how special each of us is. Your birthchart sets out your relationship with the universe, which is described in great detail not only at birth, but constantly unfolding throughout your life. I regard the birthchart as your highest self on paper, the blueprint for your life. It determines your unique pattern of gifts, strengths and challenges, and the likely timing of key experiences emerging in your life too.

I'm very often asked why the exact birthtime is so important – isn't the day enough information? Well no it isn't, as the Earth is constantly spinning in space, and that means that the constellations both on the eastern horizon of the Earth and directly overhead are changing rapidly, at the speed of approximately (varies by season) one degree of the circle for every four minutes on the clock. Therefore there are 1,440 possible birthcharts in any one day for each specific location, as that is the number of minutes in a day. They each give different 'clock faces' or orientations for the birthchart, which matter a great deal in terms of the meaning for your life. For instance, if someone is eight minutes 'wrong', in error, on their birthtime, I could be up to three years in error in how I am seeing their unfolding development in the future. So accurate information can only be given by using an accurate birthtime.

So your birthchart is determined by the time, date and place of your birth, and you can download a free birthchart from my website at www.pamgregory.com, right now. Make very sure that you enter your birth data correctly, or you will constantly be working from the wrong information.

Your birthchart is like a beautiful mandala, with strange-looking symbols and geometry; this is your lifetime map, or as I prefer to call it, your unique sheet of music. This book will not attempt to explain all of your chart, as that is a vast topic, but will outline some of the necessary elements for your understanding within the context of this book.

You will notice that there are two 'axes' to the chart; a horizontal one, and a vertical one, like crosswires in a compass. The nine o'clock position on the horizontal axis is the 'point of incarnation', more commonly known as the Ascendant. Interestingly, the ancient peoples believed that this is the point where your soul enters the body, and it is the most important point in your entire chart. This will be in a particular degree of a sign, and that sign will be the constellation that is rising on the eastern horizon at the time of your birth. This is the start of your birthchart. It may have 'Ascendant' written there, or 'Asc', or just an 'A', or even just a bold line going across the chart horizontally, but this Ascendant represents the lens through which you see the world and the world sees you; it is like a filter, and personally I feel it is much more important than your Sun sign, as it colours your entire chart. So you may have many planets in fire signs (Aries, Leo, Sagittarius), but if your Ascendant is in a water sign, such as Cancer or Pisces, it will soften the way you come across to people so you are less fiery. Equally, if you have several planets in water signs (Cancer, Scorpio, Pisces), but have an Aries (fiery) Ascendant, you will come across more vigorously and in a more 'driven' way than your water planets would otherwise suggest. This is the beginning of perceiving a constant synthesis of meaning we go through in understanding our birthcharts.

The Ascendant is linked to our identity, and the whole Ascendant-Descendant horizontal axis is one of relationship; our important one-to-one romantic relationships, but also more broadly our relationship with the public, and the world. The diagram below shows just the outer ring of a typical birthchart, and the horizontal and vertical axes. The chart below also shows each of the signs and their symbols.

The top of the vertical axis is known as the MC, the 'Medium Coeli' or middle of the sky in Latin, or more commonly as the Midheaven. This is connected to your work, your career, your social status (married, single, divorced, and transits to that point can indicate changes in those), and your reputation, but at a deeper level it is connected to your life path, where you are headed, and the values you aspire to. It also represents one of the parents, usually your mother. The opposite end, the base of the vertical line, is known as the IC, and this describes the home base, our early home life, our roots, and a parent; usually the father.

These two axes are the most sensitive points in the whole birthchart, particularly the Ascendant and Midheaven points.

This is simply an example chart. Your own birthchart will have a different orientation to this.

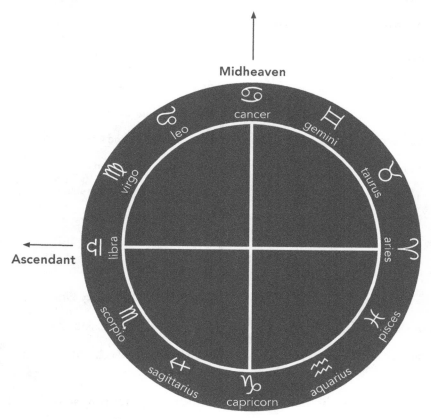

So your birthchart begins at the Ascendant, the nine o'clock position, and then moves **anti-clockwise** through each of the signs. It's worthwhile referring back regularly to the table below, which shows the signs, their 'glyphs', and the dates when the Sun is passing through these signs. You certainly don't have to memorise the dates, but it is helpful to know which sign follows which. The reason for this is that each sign contains 30 degrees, moving from 0 to 30, in an anti-clockwise direction. The degrees that will be in numbers will have a little circle to the top right of them, like a temperature degree signature (°) and then there are 60 minutes in each degree, which are indicated by a small 'tick' to the top right of the number. For the purposes of what we'll be doing in this book, don't worry about the minutes, the degrees are quite sufficient to work with.

The signs move in **anti-clockwise** direction around the birthchart, so the chronology of these through the year is listed below.

Astrological Sign	Symbol	Dates
Aries	♈	March 21st – April 19th
Taurus	♉	April 20th – May 20th
Gemini	♊	May 21st – June 20th
Cancer	♋	June 21st – July 22nd
Leo	♌	July 23rd – August 22nd
Virgo	♍	August 23rd – September 22nd
Libra	♎	September 23rd – October 22nd
Scorpio	♏	October 23rd – November 21st
Sagittarius	♐	November 22nd – December 21st
Capricorn	♑	December 22nd – January 19th
Aquarius	♒	January 20th – February 18th
Pisces	♓	February 19th – March 20th

Then there is another framework in the birthchart, again starting at the Ascendant and moving anti-clockwise. These are the 'houses' or areas of life in the chart, and they are like 12 slices of a pie. It is unlikely that these slices will be of equal size (for complex reasons to do with the way time and space is divided), but you can accept what you get from my website as being correct. Also it is unlikely that the houses in your chart will start at the beginning of signs; that rarely happens.

The divisions of the houses are called cusps, and show the beginning of each house, so the Ascendant marks the beginning of the first house, and so on. You may even have two house cusps within the same sign, which would mean that in another area of your chart you will 'jump' a sign. This would mean that you wouldn't have any house cusps in that sign. That's all okay. If the divisions between the houses aren't clear enough, draw them in more boldly so you don't have to rework it every time you look at your chart. Then I would actually number the houses in your chart, as shown in the diagram below so you don't get muddled, and then you only have to do this once.

Here is a simple expression of the house meanings:

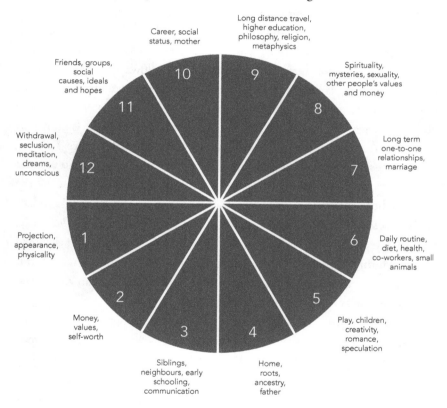

Your entire birthchart with its many variables has an enormous amount of information about who you are. However, teaching you everything about the vast subject of astrology is beyond the scope of this book, and so I am going to focus on what I increasingly believe represents the core essence of you. We will not be exploring your whole birthchart, as there are up to 3,000 variables in each birthchart, and they operate as a series of interlocking matrices, forming a complex hologram of meaning. In a full astrological consultation, all of this would be discussed. However this study takes many years for an individual to master, so here we are doing something that every reader can accomplish easily by reading this book, yet still understand themselves much more deeply than ever before. It holds the key to not only who you are, but why you are here on Earth, and what your purpose is. By the end of reading this book you will have a much clearer understanding of this.

So we're going to focus on what I feel is the most profound part of your birthchart, something known as the Nodal Axis. The Nodal Axis has a north end, a North Node, and a south end, a South Node. In the birthchart, the North Node is shown like a pair of headphones like this: ☊. Normally the South Node is not shown in your chart, but it is always directly opposing your North Node, as they form an axis. If it is marked in your chart, the South Node is shown by the headphones symbol, but upside down, so it looks more like a horseshoe: ☋. In Vedic (Indian) astrology, the North Node is known as the Dragon's Head, and the South Node is known as the Dragon's Tail. We will be focusing on this axis in this book, as it is a vital element of who you are.

Whenever I hold an astrological consultation, I have a sense of the sacred. I believe that there is something deep and magical that takes place in those sessions, that the client feels their soul journey is being crystallised and validated. Over the last few years, I have become increasingly fascinated by the Moon's Nodes, which represent in my view the most mysterious and profound element of the secret language of astrology that can give a clear sense of purpose and intention for this lifetime.

To be honest, in the early days I knew very little about the Nodes when I was studying astrology. Very little was taught, and views on the Nodes seemed confusing or contradictory. For the first 30 years or so of my practice, I largely ignored them. It has only been over the last decade that I have observed how the Nodal Axis operates in clients' charts, and have found that this is where the deepest sense of self and purpose lies, for they operate at the *soul* level. Other parts of the birthchart can operate more obviously at the psychological level; for example Mercury is how you think and communicate, determined by sign and house. So Mercury in Gemini is quick, dextrous, verbal, articulate, and may have linguistic talent, whereas Mercury in Scorpio has a deep and penetrating forensic mind, and is typically very good at research. Mars is your energy and assertiveness, again modified by sign and house, but it is very clear that if you have Mars in Aries you tend to have a 'warrior' disposition, of physicality, need to be first and be the best, whereas Mars in Pisces would express in a much gentler and more feeling way, as Pisces is a water sign. These planets operate at the *psychological* and *personality* level.

The transits of the planets operate in a visceral way; we *feel* them. For instance, a Mars transit can energise us and make us more assertive. Uranus transits can make us wired, slightly hyper and restless, and it's often harder to sleep; I often feel 'plugged into the mains' with these. The energy is more electric. Saturn transits are very different; we can feel tired, burdened, responsible, and often have a lot of work that we have to deal with, and we can feel the weight of that. Neptune transits can make us feel drifty, dreamy, spacey and often very creative, that we want to meditate more and be in an altered state. So all of these are physically felt. However, you don't *feel* the Nodes in a physical sense. They are more subtle, and seem to operate at the level of your soul's essence.

So we're not going to deal with these 'louder', more obvious and in a psychological sense more dominant parts of your chart here, we are going to be looking at one of the quietest parts of your birthchart that constitutes the compass for your soul's growth and purpose in this life. This part does not dictate your career, although it may have influence on that; but what is important is that these qualities that will be described for you in subsequent chapters for your own birthchart are expressed in some way in your life; these are behaviours and abilities that need to be developed for you to truly have a sense of purpose and fulfilment in your life. You need to have a feeling of moving towards these North Node qualities, and in doing so they become your essence. So it is less about what you 'do', and more about your essential qualities that you live every day. This is what your soul path is about in this life. However the Nodes are subtle, hard to articulate, and are whispers from the soul. It is often only when they are described by an astrologer that clients can suddenly shift level. They have a strong sense of recognition and resonance, but would have found it hard to define them clearly themselves. The Nodal Axis represents the potential for your soul's evolution.

This axis forms your treasure trove; this is where your sense of purpose and fulfilment lies. It not only explains the skills, talents and abilities with which you entered this life, but *why* you came into this life. For many astrologers, the Nodal Axis represents the 'soul contract': what you came here to do in this lifetime. I think this is one of the biggest questions that most people have, and this is often the reason why people consult astrologers as they are looking for a sense of purpose: 'What am I meant to be doing in this life?', and 'Why am I here?' I believe that understanding your Nodal Axis gives the answer to this. In Vedic astrology, the Nodes represent the most powerful part of your birthchart.

Let us just take a breath and explain exactly what the Moon's Nodes are. They are not planets, or even solid points in the cosmos. They are simply points in space, and represent where the Moon cuts the ecliptic (the Earth's path around the Sun) as it bobs and weaves slightly above and below the ecliptic (as the Moon's orbit is tilted at about five degrees to that of the Earth). So the Moon is making 'stitches', if you like, in the ecliptic, as it crosses from the south to the north once a month, then from the north to the south once a month. It is a bobbing or stitching action, and the Nodes are formed at these crossing points. The word Node means 'knot'. The Nodes move backwards through the zodiac, unlike the planets, which are generally moving forward (apart from brief retrograde periods).

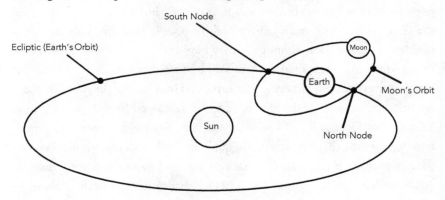

Think of the Nodes as an axis, so your North Node will always, *always*, be opposite your South Node. If your North Node is at 2° of Cancer, then your South Node will be at 2° of Capricorn, exactly opposite. The South Node is not always shown on the birthchart, but just know that it is 180° away. As we will see, this is how they operate in your life, as an axis feeding back and forward. This intersection of the ecliptic by the Moon creates an electromagnetic disturbance each time, and it is fascinating to know that these 'Nodes' are strong magnetic points, energetically. It is as if our soul is 'magnetised' towards our destiny, at a profound level.

Don't worry if you don't understand the precise astronomy of this – the important thing to know is that we all have a Nodal Axis in our birthchart, comprised of a North Node and a South Node. This axis is incredibly important in Hindu astrology, which presupposes reincarnation. The reason for this is that the South Node represents the accumulated skills, talents and abilities which have been developed over many lifetimes, and which we each bring into this life. It is a point by sign and house in our birthchart of familiarity, ease, something we can easily fall back into as a skill or behaviour pattern. It represents our instinctive comfort zone, the pull of the past, but if we operate just around our South Node all our lives we stay small.

The North Node is where we need to head towards; it is where we are supposed to develop new skills, abilities and talents that so far are undeveloped. This can feel challenging as it is unfamiliar territory, but the North Node brings with it our sense of purpose in this life, and rich fulfilment; it is the direction for your soul growth, it is evolutionary. The more we can focus our efforts on the North Node, the more we will be richly rewarded in our efforts. All the lifetimes of experience represented by the South Node by sign and house give us a strong foundation for our soul to build upon in this lifetime, but because those talents, strengths and behaviours are familiar, if we continue to fall back on them without making progress towards our North Node by sign and house, our lives will not flow as easily, nor will as much soul growth take place. The progress towards our North Node represents the process of what Jung called 'individuation'.

After extensive Indian and esoteric study, the great astrologer Dane Rudhyar wrote in his book *The Astrology of Personality*: "If we should lie along the Nodal Axis we would look into the future facing North, and accept the past facing South. The North Node deals, therefore, with the work to be done, the new accomplishment, the new faculty to be developed; and if we are willing to exert ourselves in that direction, from it we shall receive power in abundance. The South Node represents the work that has been done, the well-known accomplishment, the routine performance already gone through many times.[11]"

Although we instinctively may want to fall back onto our South Node as those habits are easy for us to practise, life will just not work as well as we intend. It's an easy option for us to repeat these South Node habits, but it may stop us growing in other ways. Once we start to move towards our North Node, there is a step change in our progress. We will notice that although it is initially more difficult simply because it is unknown, the more we live our lives moving towards our North Node by sign and house, the better our life will work. This is the direction the divine intelligence of the universe has intended for your soul growth, this time around.

The astrologer Alexander Ruperti described the North Node as "a point of divine protection or providence or of success through the use of the spiritual will."

Therefore over the many years that I have been studying astrology, increasingly I have come to see the North Node as the *arrowhead*, the *compass needle* of what this life is about. The rest of the birthchart, all the planets in their signs and houses, then act to support that direction.

When I had that revelation, it was with a flash of blinding clarity. The conversations I had with clients that seemed to move them most deeply were when we discussed the Nodal Axis. It was such a revelation; but suddenly I could now see that the Nodal Axis, although hard to perceive as it operates from the soul level, once understood, gives the reason for that soul to be here on Earth in this lifetime. It was so satisfying for clients to understand this to not only make sense of this life, and attack it with more confidence and vigour, but to see the thread of their soul in a much bigger context.

In Hindu astrology, this lifetime is just one step on the journey. Just as the Moon forms 'stitches' in the ecliptic, bobbing north and south through the months, equally this lifetime forms a stitch in the thread of the soul's journey. It spans lifetimes, weaving a tapestry of destiny as it goes. I get goosebumps when I share this with a client, and they often fall silent in recognition. So this 'line of destiny' of the Nodal Axis between the past and future of an individual is very powerful in shaping the life. In 1936 the great astrologer Dane Rudhyar said: "The lines of the Nodes show us the direction of Destiny, the purpose of Destiny...more than anything else it shows us the 'why' of an individual life...why the particular ego was projected out of the ocean of universal life...why we are born and what for.[12]" Rudhyar felt that it was the North Node where our activities in this life will reap the greatest reward, and I have to agree with him. He also felt that your North Node represented the point of 'divine will' in your birthchart, where divine intelligence had pinpointed your evolutionary intent.

In writing this book something else came to my consciousness: your birthchart is unique, and it will never be repeated in history again, which says that all of us are special. It is the birthchart for this lifetime. However, the Nodal Axis, certainly in Vedic astrology, operates beyond just this lifetime, as the South Node brings with it the wealth of material from accumulated lifetimes. It gives us a bigger picture of the soul's journey, with this lifetime simply as one episode in that journey.

So the transits of the planets operate as powerful forces in our lives, manifesting change and events as life unfolds. However, as the Nodal Axis operates subtly, we tend to get nudges, whispers from the soul, rather than having it explained to us in red neon lights. We may have insights in dreams or meditations about the wealth of material in the South Node as well as the direction of the North Node.

Traditionally in Western astrology very little has been written about the Nodes, and what has been written tends to take the view that we must move away from our experience with the South Node, that it is a place of weakness, of default, a place of non-growth which is easy and familiar for us. I disagree. The South Node has hidden potential and wisdom. The more I study the Nodes, the more I feel that the North and South Nodes work as an axis, that just like the Moon is bobbing up and down and cutting through the ecliptic twice a month, we have to continually weave our destiny by benefitting from the experience of the South Node (which in Hindu belief encompasses many lifetimes), and integrating it into our future destiny in this life. We cannot ignore either. Why would we not use all that richness of experience? It forms the foundation of this life, that with which we enter. We need to synthesise both ends of the axis. Imagine an infinity sign, like a figure eight, weaving constantly between your North and South Nodes.

I would say almost everyone at some time asks themselves the questions: 'Who am I? Why am I here?' Analysis of the whole birthchart with a professional astrologer will go a long way to answer those questions, and is unparalleled in terms of self-understanding, but the deepest answers come from the Nodal Axis. Both the signs and houses where your Nodal Axis falls are very important for interpretation; your birthdate will give you the sign, but you will need your birthtime to get the 'houses', the areas of life in your birthchart. The answers you get are set in a larger context that go beyond this life, so you start to see a theme that may be running through many lifetimes. I have to say as I became more and more interested in understanding the Nodes deeply, I started to have insights and flashes in dreams and meditations about experiences that seemed to be connected to past lives, and sometimes even future ones. Of course I have no hard evidence of this, and have not been able to pin down any past lives to specific dates (although I have an increasingly strong sense of certain geographies and historical times where and when I may have lived), but there is a feeling of resonance and recognition. These enrich and reinforce the direction I am moving in in this life.

The insights I have had into past lives all seem to involve work with the spiritual, or sacred. I've had images of being a monk in the Himalayas in a silent order, doing beautiful and often gold-leaf calligraphy in enormous sacred texts. Incan and Egypt existences come up strongly too, with involvement in mathematics, symbolism and sacred geometry. Books, learning and metaphysical knowledge always seem to be a theme, eventually working my way up to be some kind of astrological or metaphysical authority in different cultures . My South Node is in Leo in the 9th house; Leo suggests leadership or authority. The 9th house is on one level about distant geographies, but more importantly about knowledge, learning, metaphysics, wisdom, philosophy, a reaching out to understand more of the interconnectedness of the universe. These have been themes in this life since I was about seven years of age. The 9th house is also about writing, speaking and teaching; I love to write, this is now my second book, and my corporate career was very much involved in communication and making business presentations; I have given thousands. Teaching has always been part of my previous corporate career (for 20 years I taught management people all over the world how to make more persuasive business presentations), and also taught astrology in the past. This is all linked to my 9th house South Node.

Therefore my North Node (always exactly opposite the South Node) is in Aquarius in the 3rd house. The 3rd house is to do with communication, which has defined my entire career in different forms. The 3rd house is also about bringing down high wisdom, metaphysical knowledge, from the 9th house South Node to be of practical day-to-day use for people, making it relevant in their everyday lives. It is linked to making complex material simple to understand, and disseminating it. Aquarius means that the life will tend to be non-mainstream, to focus on the alternative, which will challenge the status quo in terms of how reality is seen. It describes someone who is idealistic, and is determined to help people live those ideals practically in their lives. It means that personal needs are usually put aside to do something more humanitarian. The urge is to help people, and give them a greater vision for their lives, lift their perspective by offering an alternative view of reality. Often a significant contribution to new thinking can be made. This is what I hope this book can offer.

Those descriptions really resonate with me, as to what my life is and continues to focus on. In fact, if you pare it down to the simplest essence of who I am and what my purpose is in this life, I would say that the Nodal Axis feels like a bullseye in terms of accuracy. Of course the more understanding you have of the rest of the birthchart enables you to have a richer picture of who you are. Add in the meaning of your Ascendant sign, and your Sun and Moon by house and sign, if you are confident of them. However, once you understand your Nodal Axis, the rest of your chart appears to act as support for your life direction. The other planets in your chart follow the direction of the 'arrowhead' of the North Node. It throws your life into high relief, as if you've glimpsed the underlying focal point of your blueprint.

For instance, my Sun rules the 9th house, reinforcing the themes described above for the South Node (see my birthchart below). The ruler of my Ascendant (Pluto) is also in the 9th house. My Moon is in the 3rd house of communication, writing, speaking and teaching, and is conjunct a Royal Star called Fomalhaut, the symbolism of which is the spiritual teacher. Uranus, the planet ruling Aquarius (my North Node sign), is the planet most linked to astrology, and in my chart it rules the 3rd house of communication. Therefore my important communication is likely to be alternative, and in my case, astrological. Mercury, the planet of communication, is emphasised in my chart, and directly linked to my career and life path. Virgo is the sign on my Midheaven, describing my career, and is ruled by Mercury – communication again. I could go through the whole chart describing other details, but hopefully this will give you the idea that the other planets reinforce the main theme of the Nodal Axis. They are the cavalry of helpers to help you to achieve your destiny, your dharma, by helping you develop all the skills you need this time around.

So your Nodal Axis becomes your point of focus in your birthchart, the central theme of your life, but operating quietly and powerfully from a deep level.

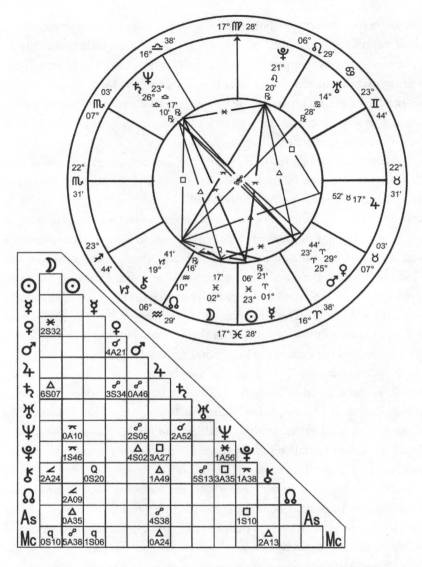

Astrological Calculations by Solar Fire software, Astrolabe Inc (www.alabe.com)

The other reason that the Nodal Axis is so important is that Eclipses can be very transformative for your development, and these can only occur when the New Moon or Full Moon falls within 18° of the transiting Nodal Axis. This is due to the Sun, Moon and Earth coming into partial or full alignment. We will be looking at this in a later chapter, when looking forward for you.

Let us now get very practical for your life. Firstly, you will need to find where your Nodal Axis is. If you haven't done so already, just download a free birthchart from my website (www.pamgregory.com). You just have to carefully enter your date, time and place of birth, and hey presto, you have your birthchart. The birthtime is very important, the more accurate the better. Remember the reason this is so important is because the Earth is continually spinning, and therefore it makes a very big difference to the orientation of the 'clock face' of the chart if the time is incorrect. We will be assigning the wrong meanings to areas of life and abilities if it is incorrect, so sadly wherever you get your birthchart from, you will need to have as accurate a time as possible.

If you are unfamiliar with astrology, this birthchart may look like a strange mandala, full of symbols and numbers, but don't worry, I will guide you through what you need to look for here. From now on, you are going to be working through this book with your *own unique birthchart*, just following the information. It's very simple.

If you have a slight contradiction with your Nodal Axis, such as the North Node is in Capricorn (10th sign) but in the 4th house, so the South Node is in Cancer (4th sign) in the 10th house, remember that the *sign* is more important than the *house* in interpreting these.

Now I will share with you some descriptions of the North Node through the signs and houses of your birthchart. These descriptions incorporate an understanding of the relevant South Node in each case. Be aware that I may be sharing more of the 'shadow' side of the South Node characteristics than I would normally do in a consultation, but this is to help you grow from that perception. What I mean by this is that in sharing some of the less positive or limiting sides of the South Node, it will help you to recognise these and propel you towards your North Node with understanding. You can achieve the greatest soul growth by taking the best that each end of the Nodal Axis offers you. In reading the descriptions below, it may simply be a word or a phrase that really resonates with you, and preoccupies you; this is where the treasure lies. You are now going to be working with your own alchemy. You need to participate in this process, as this is true co-creation in action in your life.

5 Whispers of Your Future Self

"Let yourself be silently drawn by the same strange pull of what you really love. It will not lead you astray."

Rumi

In this more practical section of the book, we're going to be discovering the meaning of several very important parts of your chart. **These are your North Node sign, and house; the planetary ruler of your North Node and its house position; your South Node sign, and house, and your Midheaven sign, and its planetary ruler**. So you will have several elements to amalgamate into your vision of your life path.

Initially this may sound a bit complex if you're unfamiliar with astrology, so I've devised this simple worksheet to help you. Just fill in the relevant sections as you work through the book, and you will hopefully start to see those parts of your birthchart come to life. On the form as you read through the relevant descriptions for your birthchart, start to write down any words, phrases or descriptions that resonate with you, and any other ideas that are prompted by these descriptions. As you work through the book, these will form key ingredients to start to live out your soul's evolution more clearly. In completing this worksheet, you are now starting to consciously co-create your future in line with your soul's growth.

Your Nodal Axis is not prescriptive in terms of actual career/work path, but the qualities need to be expressed in your life, which may suggest certain types of career. It is where your future growth lies. When you get to the Midheaven section, this will help you more with career direction, as it represents your career/life path/values you aspire to in this life.

		Sign/House/Ruler	Key Words/Thoughts/Ideas
North Node	Sign		
	House		
	Planetary Ruler		
	Planetary Ruler's House		
South Node	Sign		
	House		
Midheaven (MC)	Sign		
	Planetary Ruler		
If known	Ascendant Sign		
	Sun Sign / House		
	Moon Sign / House		

Let's begin by going through descriptions of each of the possible signs and house areas for your North Node that you will find in your birthchart. The signs indicate the quality of energy, and the house in your birthchart shows the areas of life where this will be expressed.

To find your North Node, look around the outer ring of your birthchart to find the headphones symbol. The South Node will be directly opposite this, even if it is not shown. See which sign the North Node falls in, and you only need to read the sign that is relevant to you from the descriptions below. Please see chart on page 54 if you are unsure of the symbols for the signs. Once you have that, remembering that the houses begin from the nine o'clock position, find the house that your North Node falls in. Again, you only need to read the section on 'house description' that is relevant to you. You can refer to the houses from the diagram on page 45, and also remember that it is unlikely that your houses will be equal in size. Just go with what the birthchart gives you.

North Node descriptions by Sign

North Node in Aries, ruled by Mars – South Node in Libra

Your South Node in Libra may make you very relationship focused; there may still be a feeling of not acknowledging your own needs and emotions, but deferring to others. In this sense you may still have a past life hangover of wanting to be dependent, relying on others, and being very over-adaptive in relationships. You may still be indecisive about your own wants and needs, but happy to compromise as long as harmony is kept in the relationship. In the past you may have been surrounded by beauty and culture, and lived in a relaxed way where you didn't drive yourself too hard, or push your individual potential.

However, the North Node in Aries requires that you start to take the initiative, and be courageous. You need to develop will. To help your soul growth, you need to start 'going it alone' to develop your individual identity, and focus on your uniqueness. This is likely to mean you have to be pioneering, independent, driving and high achieving. You may need to develop a strong degree of physicality, and need to be active and busy, perhaps even sporty when young. There is a desire for a sense of vigour, pushing oneself to the limit. Aries is the first sign of the zodiac, so this can give you a feeling of newness, forging new ground, and the adventure and excitement that comes with that. This North Node position can be the risk-taker. Aries is focused, direct, and in that sense, simple energy. It is primal. You decide what you want, unlike your more indecisive past, and find the shortest route to get there. There is natural leadership here, but Aries energy doesn't need social approval, you can just set off and climb the mountain yourself without taking others with you; this can be literal or metaphorical. Speed is part of the picture too, as Aries energy is quite impulsive and impatient. Anything you want, you tend to want *now*. The house position of your North Node will show you in which area of life this is likely to manifest.

The North Node in Aries can achieve a great deal in a lifetime, as achievement is the focus, much more than money or fame. It is also highly entrepreneurial, so often there is a desire to set up your own business (particularly if this falls in your 6th or 10th house), and it can often be pioneering in its focus, bringing something new into the world. Aries starts better than it finishes (the rest of the chart has to be taken into consideration, and any planets in fixed signs will help here; these are Taurus, Leo, Scorpio and Aquarius). The desire for newness will keep an Aries North Node constantly busy; that is how they like life to be. The need is to be an individual, and initiate.

However, the benefit of the South Node in Libra means that there can be less brashness and bluntness in dealings with others. It offers greater diplomacy, compromise, and works very well as the go-between, balancing your needs with the needs of others to achieve mutual benefit for all. This will have a better overall result than simply relying on the Aries energy that is 'me-first', 'I want to be the winner, the best, the fastest...' The South Node in Libra softens that self-focus, and makes for better social skills too. It's the polarity of 'me' versus 'us'. The weaving of both ends of the Nodal Axis can result in someone who is high achieving but gracious and diplomatic too, and therefore likely to attract people around you. You don't have to just rely on your North Node; it is helpful to benefit from the South Node skills too.

North Node in Taurus, ruled by Venus – South Node in Scorpio

In the past you may have experienced much drama and intensity in life, coming from the South Node in Scorpio. You may have been powerful and controlling, or experienced this from others. Your emotional life was likely to have been passionate, turbulent, and at times like a roller coaster, always running towards extremes. As a result of these emotions, you may have searched on deeper pathways, exploring spiritual laws, healing, and the death-life process in terms of reincarnation. There was a need to dig deep, a forensic focus to get to the bottom of things. You may have experienced the 'underside' of life in terms of sex, death and even criminal activity at an early age, or psychic impressions of these things, that set up a theme of 'intensity' for you. Strong emotions such as jealousy and possessiveness may still be present, as well as a strong sexuality and magnetism. You may instinctively have a desire to control people and situations.

The North Node in Taurus in this life should help you to seek much more peace and contentment. There could be an appreciation of beauty, and the world of form. So you may appreciate beauty in nature, or in beautiful things such as antiques, or ornaments. You may also have strongly developed senses; so there could also be a love of beautiful fabrics, all the scents and smells of the natural world, and an appreciation of the natural rhythms of the Earth. This Nodal Axis can allow you to see divinity in nature, combining the depth of your South Node in Scorpio with the instinctive tuning into the Earth's rhythms. There may be an interest in gardening and working with nature as a result. There is a natural 'green thumb' or fertility linked with this aspect, hence it can be very creative.

Food may be another area of interest, as this is the sign of the gourmet. There is a sensuality here with a North Node Taurus, rather than an intense sexuality of the South Node in Scorpio. There is generally very good business sense with a North Node in Taurus, and commonly these people work (if not in food or gardening/nature areas) with houses and land. However, Taurus energy has a good sense of *value*, and therefore may work with beautiful tangible things like fabrics and antiques, or helping people with their investments, particularly if the North Node falls in the 8th house of 'other people's money'. As Taurus energy is 'fixed Earth', depending on where this falls in your chart, this can suggest that you work with the human body using massage or some form of energy work. It is important to be financially self-sufficient too, and not rely on others for that, so avoid financial entanglements.

Financial security and self-sufficiency are usually very important here, but if you have this Nodal Axis you need to learn to balance the materialistic tendencies of Taurus with the more spiritual focus of Scorpio; what you value doesn't have to have a price tag on it, it can be priceless because of the spiritual wisdom it offers. This represents the weaving of the two ends of the axis.

Possessiveness is another quality which can be present with this axis, so try to connect with the contentment of your Taurus North Node, and release some of the intensity and tight grip of your Scorpio South Node. You need to move towards your Taurus North Node of trusting, rather than the distrust that the Scorpio South Node often demonstrates. Taurus is ruled by Venus, which is about love, and pleasure. So enjoy all the pleasures that life can offer, but the downside of Taurus can be laziness, so it is best balanced by using some of the laser focus of Scorpio to achieve things. The ancient ruler of Scorpio is Mars. Strength and a sense of purpose are other beneficial aspects of the South Node in Scorpio.

Peace, contentment, seeing beauty everywhere, and stability are the qualities that you need to head towards with a Taurus North Node. There is a feeling of wanting to keep the status quo, keeping things steady, and avoiding plunging into the crises of the past. It is important not to get pulled back into that emotional intensity, but make a concerted effort to go towards peace. Trusting the instinctive wisdom of the body is another feature of the Taurus North Node that can be cultivated.

North Node in Gemini, ruled by Mercury – South Node in Sagittarius

The South Node in Sagittarius means that you enter this life with much wisdom. You are likely to have studied metaphysical subjects, or those of higher consciousness. You may have a strong moral, religious or philosophical code as a result of this, and can easily slip into being dogmatic and 'playing God'. It is linked to the truth as you see it, and Sagittarius as a sign can easily develop an evangelistic attitude to their truth, and have an attitude of judgement from the past. This can be judging self and/or others. Together with this, there can be a bluntness, directness, and even tactlessness at times; it is the sign most associated with being judgemental and intolerant. It is also important to have your opinions recognised.

There is a fascination with the 'bigger picture', a constant desire to reach into the cosmos and explore further. Therefore there can be a restless energy with this, and perhaps an avoidance of commitment, which can be limiting. The South Node in Sagittarius has a roving, adventurous quality, so in the past you may have experienced foreign lifetimes, where you had a large degree of freedom and independence, and they will continue to be important to you. You may have developed a love for big horizons and wild instinctive places;

the free spirit, the uncivilised part of you, still runs deep. You may sense a rawness in your nature and you may have lived beyond the boundaries of normal society. In the past you may have been a philosopher, and constantly wondered and developed your visions of the interconnectedness of the universe, but rarely putting pen to paper.

Now, with the North Node in Gemini, there is a need to bring all that 'higher mind wisdom' down to reality; your task is to make it accessible to others in a simple way, breaking down the big philosophical thoughts into bite-size pieces. You are the messenger. It is about everyday communication, making it relevant to everyday life, and making it real. You need lots of constant communication through the day, and the stimulation of new ideas. There is a curiosity here, and a dexterity with language. You may be the teacher, writer, salesperson or mentor, but communication is strongly emphasised, and you will be interested in sharing this knowledge widely. If your South Node in Sagittarius is wild and uncivilised, your North Node in Gemini is much more linked to civilisation, and how this wisdom can be used practically. You may still be prone to 'blue sky thinking', but the ideas can now be used by many more people. It is about dissemination of knowledge, and breaking down complex subjects so they are comprehensible. So whether this comes via teaching, writing, speaking, blogging, making videos, that is your task this time around. You will be skilled in at least one of those areas. The focus is on communicating the wisdom that you have already acquired, rather than constantly philosophising but not sharing it with others. You may be using several different forms of communication too, using the dexterity of Gemini.

The endless curiosity of the Gemini North Node will constantly evolve the knowledge of your Sagittarius South Node, and develop it, but without being judgemental or dogmatic about it. Gemini has a greater flexibility, a lightness of touch. Gemini tends to operate within the bounds of society, as that is where the communication can be most useful, although this North Node sign always has creative non-conformism at its heart; so cultivate your own original thinking too. This axis is about the dissemination of wisdom.

North Node in Cancer, ruled by the Moon – South Node in Capricorn

In the past you worked very hard, and built your status and reputation. These were important to you. Capricorn is very conventional energy, so it brings with it pride, respectability, a sense of authority and a strong work ethic. There is always a sense of duty, tradition, conservatism, and being conscientious, and the ability to work in a hierarchy, as there is respect for authority. However, due to the excellent organisational skills of Capricorn, particularly with large projects, a Capricorn South Node may have often been the boss, the leader, of large organisations. Work and achievement were the focus, thus it is common to put personal concerns aside to achieve something significant out in the world.

Capricorn South Node brings with it a sense of ambition, being methodical, and steadily working your way up to the top. There is a steadiness of purpose here. It is very goal-oriented and practical, and may have even had to endure hardships and austerity. Perhaps in a past life you had to take responsibility for the family, as Capricorn is linked to the father archetype. Financial security for yourself and your family is very important. Frugality is often part of the picture. In the past there may have been little time for feelings or sentimentality, as the focus was providing and being responsible.

Now with the North Node in Cancer, the focus shifts to the emotional and family realm. It is no longer so much looking after the financial needs of the family, but rather the emotional needs. There may be a hankering to be out in the world and achieving, but if you do seek authority and position, you may find that life doesn't flow that well; the priority is to nurture your family, and protect them. You need to become more emotionally open and available to others, and to recognise your own need to be nurtured, as well as nurturing others. You will grow to know what they need to feel nurtured, and protected, and relax your guarded professional persona. You will come to value the importance of the emotional realm. Family, roots and heritage are valued too, the connection to the past, to history, and with a sense of belonging. There is a need with your North Node in Cancer to indulge your emotions, to very much live in them, and be much less interested in the outer world. Love needs to become more important than public recognition.

Cooking and gardening may be interests for you; commonly people with the North Node in Cancer do these things for a living (particularly if the North Node falls in the 6th or 10th houses). However, nurturing and nourishing others in general will be important to express. Cancer is the sign of 'motherhood' and even if you do not have any children of your own, you can express it in various ways. You may be a teacher, particularly of young children, or may work with special needs people, or those who need a greater amount of care. I have known several people who work as foster mothers and surrogate mothers with this Nodal position. Sometimes nursing is a way to express your 'nurturing' of others. Making others feel safe and protected, however you do this, is all part of the North Node in Cancer.

There is an instinctive understanding of the rhythms of the cosmos with a North Node in Cancer (this is ruled by the Moon, which has a pull on the tides), and your moods may be affected strongly by the Moon. There is great sensitivity here too, and the appreciation of sensitivity and vulnerability of others.

With the North Node in Cancer you can be successful if you are running a project or getting involved with a charity which cares for others, often without any financial reward.

So although you may sometimes feel a pull to be achieving in the outer world, that will not be satisfying to you, as your purpose in this life is to live in your emotions and support others. The focus is the home, not the world, and it will be important that you understand the value of that. It is also important that the emotional 'defendedness' and tightness of Capricorn melts into the emotionally available North Node in Cancer. You don't have to have a title, or run an organisation, to feel you have achieved in life. The satisfaction of protecting and caring for others can be priceless. That is the lesson of the North Node in Cancer.

North Node in Leo, ruled by the Sun – South Node in Aquarius

In the past you may have felt on the periphery of society, where your life operated outside the mainstream. Indeed, you may have challenged the views of the mainstream, as Aquarius energy will always tend to confront the status quo with new ideas. These may have been new scientific ideas, or 'alternative' ideas, but were often far-sighted. You were likely to have been highly idealistic, and will still carry that as part of your nature now. You had an originality, you may have been an innovator, and thought 'outside the box'. Equality was an important principle, and you were able to put personal goals to the side to help the common good in society. All of these qualities you will still have inside you, as part of your soul journey.

Aquarius always has a 'push-pull' around individuality and the group effort. Therefore the South Node in Aquarius person, although feeling very different from others in mainstream society, was able to sacrifice 'ego' for the higher principle of the group ideals, of contributing to society in some way. You may have been submerged in the group, rather than being recognised as a separate individual. You may also have had a cool, slightly distant intellectualism; ruled by Uranus, you may have appeared emotionally detached.

You bring with you into this life all of that idealism and humanitarian focus, but now you can be centre stage in fighting for it, and even become a leader. You are now operating within society, not from outside it. This is how the weaving of the South and North Node become so important in becoming the best you can be.

Instead of the cool intellectualism, you can now live fully from the heart, with a radiant warmth that you express to everyone. Rather than reacting against elements of society, there is an enthusiasm for life and all it can offer. There is less resistance with the Leo North Node. At times as you pull away from group activity you may feel lonely, but it is best to immerse yourself in your creative potential, for this is where you will blossom. You may have a love of play, of games and fun, and bringing joy and happiness to others; just let your light shine. There can be a real flair and style in your creativity, and unlike your South Node past when you were on the borders of society, you are very happy to be centre stage and have your individuality recognised, appreciated and applauded. So rather than immersing yourself in group activity, you need to develop a sense of leadership, courage, confidence, creativity, and inspiration for others. You have a huge generosity of spirit which draws others to you. The Leo North Node is usually very sociable, sharing with others simply for the joy of being, rather than having to debate intellectually how to improve the world. You may well work with children, either in a creative or games capacity, and always bring a sense of joy to what you do. Learn more creative individual self-expression.

You may be particularly proud of your own children, and often children of North Node in Leo parents are very successful. Much joy will come through your children.

The best way forward with the North Node in Leo is to integrate the idealism and humanitarianism that you still feel from your South Node in Aquarius, and you may still want to promote these causes; but now you are willing to step into a centre stage position, and lead and inspire others. You need to live from the heart rather than your head. This is a leaning into life rather than pulling back from the way the mainstream operates. Through your leadership and courage, you will be able to achieve something unique for humanity. In blending your South and North Nodes, you can be an innovator in society.

North Node in Virgo, ruled by Mercury – South Node in Pisces

This is a highly sensitive Nodal position. You may be sensitive physically or psychically, and sometimes find it hard to live in the world, instead preferring to pull back to places of retreat and solitude. You may find the world too overwhelming and invasive. As your energy is so sensitive, you may have boundary issues, finding it difficult to clearly delineate where you end and others begin; so this can drain your energy at times. All this comes from the past when your life may have been dreamy, drifty, or tuned into intangibles of energy, being able to sense how others are feeling beneath the words. There is great gentleness, sympathy and compassion here, and also great sensitivity to any kind of suffering. You may have experienced too much sacrifice, and may have even suffered a great deal in the past, or been incarcerated somewhere, which is why retreat can feel familiar. This is also necessary to recharge your energetic batteries. Often there is great love for animals, as the recognition of the sanctity of all life means that you feel at one with the animal kingdom too.

The past withdrawal from the world that has become so familiar to you may have been your choice, or forced upon you; but there can be a loss of ego with a Pisces South Node, as the urge is to return to the bliss of Source, the oceanic oneness. Pisces is the most ego-less sign in the zodiac. Pisces is ruled by Neptune, so it can be highly idealistic; but you may not have actually made that sense of idealism practical in the world.

That is the task of your life this time around. The Virgo North Node can be quite a taskmaster in terms of grounding your ideals and making them of practical use in the world. You can still feel idealistic, but you need to start to make these ideals more real in the world to help others; the Virgo North Node wants to be of practical service to others. So this lifetime is about being more discerning and discriminating, developing clear boundaries, and operating on the Earth plane. Sometimes the Pisces North Node person may have even indulged in drugs or substances to better achieve that elusive state of bliss (Neptune which rules Pisces is linked to drugs and addiction), but this time around the Virgo North Node is about purification and perfectionism. The Virgo-Pisces axis is considered the health axis, in that many people with this emphasis in their charts are drawn to healthcare in some capacity, partly because of the empathy and sympathy, partly because of the urge to 'purify', and partly because of the desire to be of practical service to others. Virgo energy can be very concerned with hygiene and detail; there is a precision which a Pisces South Node simply doesn't have. So they can work in laboratories in a more conventional sense, but there is likely to be a pull another way.

The Virgo North Node can commonly be drawn to alternative healing, as the Pisces South Node has an instinctive understanding of the essence of things, the gestalt, and has a deep love for nature in the sense of our holistic universe. Virgo is an Earth sign, and wants to make this deep love and understanding practical. So in integrating these two ends of the axis you can be drawn to a deep exploration of the inherent wisdom of the Earth; a feeling of being able to draw on the profound knowledge of the ancient wisdom-keepers. In this way, the Virgo North Node may develop an interest in herbs, plant medicine, essential oils, homeopathy, and energy medicine in general. There is a feeling that the Earth has everything we need to heal ourselves. Many healers have a Virgo North Node.

It is common also in nutrition and dietetics; Virgo is linked astrologically to the intestines, the gut, and of course the microbiome. This is where we have millions of tiny beneficial bacteria that are so important in our health; Virgo also rules the tiny, getting the details right. Hence there is often great interest in nutrition, and in getting the body to work more efficiently. Virgo emphasis is about *efficiency* of your whole system, and being specific as to where the blocks or problems in the body lie.

Virgo not only has a fascination with detail, but also with practical skills, hence there is often an admiration for artisan skills such as carpentry, or detailed handmade work such as embroidery or handmade clothes. That may be another way this axis can be expressed, but any artisan products are likely to be made from natural materials, in this sense of coming from the Earth.

As Virgo is ruled by Mercury, communication may be emphasised. This may be integrated with the inspired creativity of the Pisces South Node, or you may often be writing about nutrition or health matters.

So the creativity and sensitivity of the Pisces South Node becomes woven into something in this life that is more defined, grounded, and practical to be helpful for the world. You may still occasionally feel like a victim, overwhelmed with life or the problems of others, as your Pisces South Node boundaries are not strong. This is a lifetime when you are much more living in the world, and using your inspiration in a beneficial way on the Earth.

North Node in Libra, ruled by Venus – South Node in Aries

In the past you have been brave, pioneering, and independent. You may still have a strong sense of having to 'go it alone', and may have had to struggle and fight in your early life. You may have been in a leading or fighting position in previous lives, and achieved many things that required confidence and courage. There is a physicality about Aries which you may still have; a need to be on the go, physically active, a restlessness to achieve. An Aries South Node would have wanted to be the best, be the first, be the fastest, and you may have driven yourself hard, even to exhaustion, in doing that. The energy is highly self-motivated and achievement-oriented, and it may be hard now to stop that constant pushing of self.

Aries is a simple, direct, primal energy; so in the past you would have decided on a goal or something you wanted to achieve, and then just gone out and done it without thinking too much more about consequences. There was probably little thought about involving others, as you were perfectly capable and happy of being independent, and not needing social approval. Freedom and personal achievement may still feel very important to you.

However now with the North Node in Libra, this is all about involving others. This is becoming aware that by being in partnerships, co-operation and collaboration with others, you may actually produce better results than just doing it yourself. There may still be a restlessness that you could do it faster by yourself, or even a resentment of 'I have to do everything myself'. You have to become aware that by involving other people and their talents, what you achieve is much richer, but you are also social in the process, sharing with others.

It's interesting that your South Node in Aries is ruled by Mars, god of war, whereas your North Node in Libra is ruled by Venus, goddess of love and peace. So you need to soften this urgent physicality and need for speed and vigour into something more balanced. You need to develop diplomatic and social skills, rather than just forcing results. You'll need to take lots of differing viewpoints into consideration, rather than just your own. Aries can be a little selfish as it is so self-focused, and tends only to think about himself rather than others. So you are being required to temper the impulsiveness and impatience, and spend the time to listen to others, and accept that their viewpoints may have value too. It is 'we' versus 'you'. So there is a slowing down here too, with this Nodal Axis. You will have a strong presence from all your self-willed activity of the past, but it's important not to be in continual fight mode, but rather one of co-operation and openness. The focus shifts from assertion to peace, which is linked to Venus in its rulership of Libra.

So with the North Node in Libra, you need to develop a sense of equilibrium, gracefulness, and being socially adept so you don't dominate, but always manage to find the midpoint of compromise which is satisfactory to everyone. You no longer have to drive through with your way of doing things; it is a shared effort. In this sense you can relax more, enjoy the journey, and take your foot off the accelerator. You'll need to develop diplomacy, tact, and some sensitivity to others, as your path in this life is more inclusive and balanced. You may even start to feel the pleasure that this brings that it isn't just you driving everything, as the feeling of sharing can give you much support. You can lose some of your 'fight', and focus more on balancing all sides in any situation. In fact, you will ideally become more concerned about others' points of view than your own, as Libra is the sign of being 'other-directed', waiting to see how everyone else feels and reacts to something before you decide yourself.

This is a big change from the past, as you start to want justice, fairness and peace for all. In being ruled by Venus, your North Node is more feminine in its expression than your South Node past. You can develop an elegance, grace, and popularity with this position as it is very socially focused. The South Node in Aries may still give you the drive, focus and sense of achievement to make things happen, and Libra is also a cardinal sign of action, but you will be doing things with a sense of beauty, balance and peace. You may even be drawn to the arts and culture with this axis too, or involved in work as the go-between and the diplomat.

North Node in Scorpio, ruled by Pluto – South Node in Taurus

In the past you may have had to focus on survival issues, and you may still carry a lot of intensity with you. Problems may take on a life-or-death focus for you. The need for physical resources and financial security to feel safe may be a strong drive for you, illustrated by your South Node in Taurus. This South Node position instinctively wants to accumulate tangible, physical things including money to give you a feeling of material security and safety. So it can be quite acquisitive; things matter, and as Taurus is ruled by Venus, you may have a love of beautiful things, and valuable things. There may also be a love of the pleasures of life, the physical and sensual indulgence of delicious food and beautiful surroundings; you may still have acutely developed senses, particularly touch. You may bring into this life much creativity and a strong sense of beauty.

Taurus is the sign most associated with laziness and indulgence, and likes to keep things as they are, without too many shocks or surprises. This is often due to feeling insubstantial or insecure in early life, in previous incarnation(s). It is easy to get stuck in old ways of being as a result, and accumulate beautiful things for their own sake, or to give a sense of permanence, solidity and security.

Both Scorpio and Taurus are concerned with value. Taurus sees value more in physical, tangible terms, whereas Scorpio is focused on what is beneath the surface. A North Node in Scorpio brings penetrating insight into others and an understanding of other people's values. On one level this North Node can be drawn to helping others with their money and investments, as Scorpio is linked in the natural horoscope to the 8th house, which is 'other people's money'. It brings with it the South Node in Taurus understanding of the value of physical and financial assets. However, generally the North Node in Scorpio likes to dig beneath the surface, and see life in a deeper way. There is a draw towards the spiritual, the esoteric, and alternative healing modalities. The North Node in Scorpio generally sees greatest value in the non-physical rather than the physical.

Very often with a South Node in Taurus and a North Node in Scorpio I have seen that the person experiences a point in life where there is a big financial loss, or certainly where possessions have to be given up. This is to take them onto a deeper level of understanding, which is demanded by the North Node in Scorpio. Scorpio is the sign of transformation, and this is likely to occur in the area of what is valued. The spiritual, rather than the physical, needs to become the focal point of value. That is often when there is an acceleration in learning about spiritual laws.

This can take many forms; it may be a fascination with the death/transformation process, and you may be drawn to work with the dying in that powerful moment of transition (Scorpio is ruled by Pluto, planet of death and transformation). You may study forms of energy/alternative healing, or have a love of yoga and t'ai chi. There is an appreciation of the profound wisdom and energetics of the body. These pursuits also weave the Taurean love of nature and the Earth from the South Node into an organic view with the North Node in Scorpio. There is an instinctive understanding brought from the past, with the South Node in Taurus, that there is a connection between everything in the universe.

There is a need to penetrate, dig deep, be forensic, to get to the bottom of matters. This is terrific for research. Whereas the South Node in Taurus may create resistance to change, as Scorpio's ancient ruler is Mars, there is a greater feeling of forward motion and laser-beam focus with the North Node in Scorpio. There is a desire to transform self on a regular basis, to go through different episodes in life where the old self is shed, and a deeper, wiser self is born. There is enormous willpower, magnetism and presence with the North Node in Scorpio. Any indulgences from the South Node in Taurus are left behind, as Scorpio is one of the, if not the most, disciplined of all the signs. The house area of the North Node will show where this focus and discipline will be applied.

Security with this Nodal Axis comes from knowledge, rather than possessions.

North Node in Sagittarius, ruled by Jupiter – South Node in Gemini

The Nodal Axis here is concerned with communication and dissemination of knowledge. In the past, you may have picked up a lot of knowledge via social interaction, but this can be 'lower mind' information that comes from chatter. Gemini can be quite magpie-like in the way it accumulates information – a little here, a little there – which can give breadth but not necessarily depth. Now you have to take that knowledge, and develop wisdom, or 'higher mind' information. This transformation comes via the connection with meaning. Once you start to give all your information meaning, deeper relevance, then you can start to develop a philosophy or belief system. A sense of idealism is part of the North Node in Sagittarius; freedom and the search for truth are very important, and you can feel like a free spirit, being happiest in wild instinctive places.

There is a tendency from the past with the South Node in Gemini to be scattered and at times indecisive. Now you have to put that knowledge into a more coherent form, and there is a need to develop a bigger picture, a wider vision for that information. Both Gemini and Sagittarius can be restless and roving, as they are both mutable signs. Travel may be a way that you find more knowledge, as it stimulates this 'bigger picture'. What is required is less chatter and distraction, and a more focused drive towards an understanding of higher consciousness and the interconnectedness of the universe. You'll constantly be searching for truth and meaning in everything. It is important to try to resist distraction, particularly of the social kind. Try to move from a scattered mind and find stillness in yourself, in order for your wisdom to be developed.

You will naturally be an adventurer, explorer and visionary; developing an instinct about the future is an important part of the North Node in Sagittarius. You are likely to be a natural teacher, and able to inspire curiosity in others. It may become important to you to achieve the right qualifications and credentials for your work, as it ensures more respect for your opinions, which are likely to be strong. However, it is also important to fulfil your North Node in Sagittarius so that you actually record your wisdom, put pen to paper, and don't just keep roaming as a free spirit but leaving no legacy. This then incorporates your South Node in Gemini.

The South Node in Gemini may be drawn to city life and civilisation, whereas the North Node in Sagittarius needs to be in wilder, freer, natural places. There will a constant desire through life for self-improvement and personal growth, for self and others.

The North Node in Sagittarius, despite the fact it is a 'mutable' (flexible) sign, can become dogmatic or even evangelistic about the TRUTH, as you see it. The benefit of weaving the South Node in Gemini into this is that Gemini brings objectivity and lightness to a subject, even wit, so it can pull back the tendency to 'play God'. The South Node can also help the developing wisdom of the North Node in Sagittarius as it learns much from acute objective observation of people and situations. This can help any potential judgement or intolerance of the North Node in Sagittarius. The North Node in Sagittarius has more of a singular, pioneering quality, so at times you may miss the social buzz of your South Node in Gemini; but you have a bigger vision and purpose in this life.

North Node in Capricorn, ruled by Saturn – South Node in Cancer
The South Node in Cancer gives a tendency to be preoccupied with personal and emotional concerns of self and others, particularly close family. There is a natural pull to live in the emotions and feelings of others, and be nurturing,

supportive and protective towards them. As Cancer is the sign of motherhood, there is a natural maternal instinct here, a love of children, and that may still strongly manifest in this life. There may also be a tendency to mother others.

The family is usually the focus of the past, and what gives a sense of emotional security. The South Node in Cancer can suggest a tendency to collapse back into child mode, with all the sensitivity and vulnerability that goes with that. There can be too much preoccupation to what others think and say about you or your loved ones, and you can take these things in an over-sensitive way. There may be a preoccupation with helping others with their personal problems. Sentimentality may be part of the picture, as Cancer is one of the signs most connected to the past, history, and family roots and tradition. So there is a 'pulling back to the past' element to the South Node in Cancer, but it also makes you value your heritage too. You may even use family problems as an excuse as to why you can't take on more responsibility, or be out in the world more.

As the Moon rules Cancer, moods can fluctuate, and this tendency can still leak through in this life. There is a need to develop stronger boundaries and an emotional steadiness. As the Moon is also concerned with nurturing others, this can take the form of nourishing others; Cancer is the sign highly associated with cooking and catering, a literal feeding of others. Or you may wish to make a profession where you are caring for others in their own homes; however, although valuable, that is 'falling back' towards your South Node, rather than moving towards your North Node.

The North Node in Capricorn requires a reorientation of focus from living in the feelings and being preoccupied with the emotional well-being of the family and loved ones, to go beyond your personal life and work at financial security for yourself and the family. There is also a need to avoid pulling back to safe, supportive ground of home, and strike out in the world to achieve. The North Node in Capricorn means that you need to develop ambition, focus, and aim high. You need to become ambitious, goal-oriented, and focus on achievement and success, even if this takes time to build. You should have natural organising abilities, and be able to take on big projects. You have the potential to climb to a high position, as you are able to work with or for big businesses and institutions. The North Node in Capricorn needs to develop natural authority, the ability to handle responsibility in a mature way, and be disciplined, focused and practical. Status and reputation will be important, and it is very common for the North Node in Capricorn to become the head of large organisations. Therefore any vulnerable childlike feelings must be put to one side, as you start to move towards your North Node and become a valuable player out in the world, someone who is more concerned with financial security and providing than being involved in emotional issues. In this life you are the provider, the responsible one, rather than the nurturer.

You need to believe in yourself, be confident of your abilities, and not collapse back into your family for support, for in this life it is you who are likely to be supporting others. Personal needs and emotions are put to one side, and with your enviable persistence and endurance you are likely to produce impressive results. The house area where your North Node falls will show you the area where this strong achievement is likely to manifest.

North Node in Aquarius, ruled by Uranus – South Node in Leo

In the past you may have experienced a strong sense of individuality and creativity, and you will still benefit from that in this life. You may still carry a presence and confidence, as in the past you were likely to have been 'centre stage' in some capacity, and operating within mainstream society. The South Node in Leo brings with it some wonderful warm, radiant, generous, loving heart energy; but it can at the same time be quite ego-focused, as you may have achieved admiration in the past for what you achieved.

The North Node in Aquarius demands that you put personal concerns and ego to one side, this time around. There is a much greater sense of idealism here. Aquarius has the tendency to operate from the intellect, whereas a weaving together of the South Node Leo heart energy would be helpful to balance this. Rather than being in the centre of society, the North Node in Aquarius is drawn to operate from the periphery, to question current norms. The drive is always to challenge the status quo, and aid evolution in that way. There is even a desire to court social rejection, to deliberately not accept mainstream views. Therefore you may be drawn to alternative and scientific leading-edge concepts and ideas.

Freedom and independence are very important to you with a North Node in Aquarius, and you must leave behind any desire for the limelight and centre stage position of the South Node in Leo. You have a bigger humanitarian vision now, there is a desire to improve the lot of mankind in some way (defined by the house position of the North Node) and promote an ideal. This is very likely to be a non-mainstream ideal. This ideal could dominate your life, and the North Node in Aquarius is able to produce something truly significant and evolutionary for the world. A sense of activism is to be encouraged, and an ability to be far-sighted and even visionary. There may be a touch of the rebel in you, and you can be 'ahead of your time'.

Although there can still be a pull back to your South Node in Leo of 'what about me as an individual', the drive must be towards the group ideal. This is a more impersonal existence, and indeed you may feel as if you are an innovator or even a rebel, operating on the outskirts of society, and nor is your individuality necessarily recognised within the group or the ideal, but rather submerged into it. Your sense of meaning comes from the collective and the group ideals; your sense of being part of a like-minded tribe needs to become more important than celebrating your own individual achievements. You may feel that you are a vehicle or messenger for new, different points of view to be incorporated into society, for the greater good of all; you are someone who sees ideas differently from the mainstream.

You may still at times have a pullback to luxurious living, and pleasurable comforts of life. However, the North Node in Aquarius has a much greater sense of mission, and would consider such luxuries to be an indulgence, and a divergence from your sense of idealism, with the need to improve the collective. Aquarius has a focus on the collective and community.

You can still benefit not only from some of the warmth and heart energy of the South Node of Leo, but also the confidence that was learned in the past. This may enable you to stand your ground when challenged by the mainstream. You may have even been an authority or leader of some kind in the past, and carry that natural magnetism now. All of this past experience will benefit the potentially impersonal and intellectual North Node in Aquarius. The focus is humankind, rather than the self.

North Node in Pisces, ruled by Neptune – South Node in Virgo

You may enter this life with great humility and a strong sense of service. Virgo is one of the most humble signs, as there is often anxiety about self-worth here; the perfectionism of the South Node in Virgo can mean that you are just never good enough. So this can bring a low-level fretting, a restlessness to help others, a preoccupation with practical details, and a constant desire to discriminate, separate and analyse, which can bring a worrying nature. There may still be an obsessive tendency around creating order and efficiency, and even workaholic tendencies that have to be resisted. You may have obsessions around hygiene or health, and the constant need for mental input (as Virgo is ruled by Mercury, planet of communication) can be tiring; it's important to find time to relax and just surrender.

However, in the past you are likely to have developed some outstanding skills around detail and a sharp mind; you will always want things to be practically useful, and there can be a love of artisan skills, as well as anything handmade. Virgo is an Earth sign, so the South Node in Virgo can bring a solid groundedness. You may have worked as an artisan, a healer, clinician or doctor in the past, and you may have already gained knowledge about healing; you may have even worked with Earth energies in the past.

However, the need is to go towards the North Node in Pisces, which is about the oneness of all things, rather than the division into compartments. It celebrates the holistic and connected nature of all things, and rather than being of practical service, it sees itself as being spiritually inspiring. If you have the North Node in Pisces, you can see beauty in all things, and the unity of everything. You need to surrender to the oceanic oneness of all-beingness, and connect back to Source. There is a feeling of letting go here, and being of spiritual service, rather than practical service. It is about inspiration rather than discrimination.

You may have a particular sensitivity to animals, seeing all sentient beings as part of the oneness of life. Whether with humans or animals, there is likely to be great sensitivity to energy. You may feel other people's energy, and that of animals too, and easily be able to tune into this as your intuition is so acute. You may work as an energy healer. This Nodal Axis is common too in the charts of more conventional healers, such as nurses.

If you have the North Node in Pisces you will be less concerned with the details, and more concerned with the creativity and inspiration of life. Often a North Node in Pisces finds these things hard to articulate; there just aren't the right words for it – it is a feeling that can't necessarily be explained, just a feeling of bliss. If you have a North Node in Pisces you need to develop the qualities of gentleness, compassion, understanding, empathy and sensitivity to all suffering. Its urge is to embrace all of life, rather than analyse it with all its faults. There is a sense of surrendering to a higher level of being when the North Node in Pisces is operating at its best.

If you are pulled towards working with Earth energies, which may be a residue from the past, you can put this ability towards excellent use in going towards your North Node in Pisces, as that will add spiritual inspiration to your very specific knowledge. It may be working with energy itself, or herbs, or essential oils. There is a sense that the Earth, with its ancient wisdom, has everything we need to heal.

So if you have the North Node in Pisces, you need to develop a life that is expressing creativity, imagination, healing or spirituality in some form in order to be evolving your soul growth. You need to move away from the details and specifics of your South Node in Virgo, where things had to be nailed down very precisely. You may have led a very work-oriented and disciplined life in the past, but now need to live more in the flow of life, in all its beauty and breathtaking oneness. You need to be aware of the sense of unconditional love which is offered by the North Node in Pisces, and develop that sense of connection with the divine; there is a need to touch the ethereal in life, rather than the detail. You will stop finding fault with others, and the world, and accept all that is. It's about moving from the critical mind to the universal mind.

As both Virgo in its humility and Pisces in its lack of ego can suffer from doubt and insecurity, part of you may still feel that. Those feelings are the lower level of expression of the signs, but the higher level of Pisces expression with the North Node is surrendering to divine oneness: 'let go and let God'. More than any other sign, the Pisces North Node always sees love as the answer.

House Position of the Planet ruling your North Node

Now you know which sign your North Node falls in, another very important part of the jigsaw that you are putting together is which house (area of life in your birthchart) the ruling planet of your North Node falls. At the end of this section you'll find the 'rulerships' of the signs by each of the planets, as each sign is ruled by a planet. This will give you another rich piece of information. For me, as I have an Aquarius North Node, the ruler of Aquarius is Uranus; and Uranus in my birthchart happens to fall in my 8th house of deep spiritual matters. Uranus has very particular symbolism, and is the planet most associated with astrology. It is the maverick, the outsider, someone who doesn't operate within the mainstream, but challenges the status quo. It rules my 3rd house of communication as that's where the Aquarius cusp falls in my chart, as I mentioned earlier. So it reinforces the North Node theme that I will be a communicator for an alternative subject (in my case, astrology) that has deep spiritual content, that isn't fully embraced – at least yet – by the mainstream. Bullseye! I'm living my purpose.

So be sure to find out the house that the planet that rules your North Node sign is falling in. Firstly you find the sign of your North Node, then identify that sign's planetary ruler from the symbols below, then simply find where that planet falls in the 'houses' of your birthchart.

In building your astrological vocabulary here, the pieces of information may be very simple, but when put together they should resonate deeply with you, and give you insights as to how you can consciously construct your future self.

Here is a list of the planets, and the signs they rule:

Planet	Symbol	Ruled Sign(s)
Sun	☉	Leo
Moon	☽	Cancer
Mercury	☿	Gemini and Virgo
Venus	♀	Taurus and Libra
Mars	♂	Aries
Jupiter	♃	Sagittarius
Saturn	♄	Capricorn
Uranus	♅	Aquarius
Neptune	♆	Pisces
Pluto	♇ ♇	Scorpio

I often say that each planet is like a multi-faceted diamond. This is because although you can specify one keyword to each planet – for instance Jupiter is expansion, Saturn is contraction – there are many potential expressions of that core meaning. So here is a useful reference table for you, to deepen your knowledge.

☉	Sun	Quality and expression of energy (changes by sign), soul purpose, central sense of self, joy, enthusiasm, life force, power centre. Gold. Heart and back.
☽	Moon	Instinctive emotional reactions, the mother, home, what you need to feel instinctively comfortable, moods, feelings, dominant needs, ying energy, daily rhythm. Protectiveness and need for nurturing. Sensitivities. Stomach and breasts, female hormones.
☿	Mercury	Communication, mind-set, perception and observation, intellect, knowledge, early schooling, siblings, thinking. Nervous system, lungs and hands.
♀	Venus	Love, contentment, self-valuation. Sense of beauty, artistry, creativity, flair, charm. Urge to co-operate and adapt, gracefulness, gentleness. Indulgence, love of creature comforts. In a man's chart, the kind of woman he'd be attracted to. Lower back, kidneys, throat.
♂	Mars	Energy, drive, ambition, entrepreneurial spirit, physicality, assertion, aggression, sex drive, goals, focus. Pioneering, courageous, forceful, passionate. In a woman's chart can indicate the kind of man she would be attracted to. Inflammation, injuries. Iron, blood, head.
♃	Jupiter	Expansion, self-improvement, generosity, joviality, education, training, teaching, publishing, law, religion, philosophy. Higher mind and consciousness—raising subjects. Long distance travel. Optimism, confidence, gambling. Liver, hips, thighs, growths, corpulence.

	Saturn	Limitation, contraction, blockage, delay, time, ageing, father figure, responsibility, maturity, ambition, depression, patience, practicality, controlled, cautious, serious. Hard work, burdens, fear, endings. Authority figures, government. Status quo. Teeth, bones, knees, skin, lead, boundaries.
	Uranus	Rebellion, revolution, restless, disruptive energy, the maverick, breaks the rules, freedom, individual self-expression, truth, honesty, creativity, originality, intensity. Autocratic, outspoken, unconventional. Ankles and circulation, breaks, mutations. Uranium.
	Neptune	Altered states, meditation, unconditional love, healing, dreams, telepathy, spirituality, idealism, sensitivity, vagueness, confusion, deception, disappointment, things not being what they seem. Transcendence, imagination, inspiration, romance. Allergies, leaky gut syndrome. Deficient blood, fluids in the body, lymphatic system, feet.
♇P	Pluto	Endings and beginnings, death and rebirth, transformation, empowerment, regeneration, intensity, stress, fundamental change, feeling fated. Jealousy, possessiveness, control, manipulation, invasion, criminal activity, underworld, primal, sexual, compulsive, unconscious, catharsis. Sexual organs, elimination. Mental illness. Plutonium.

House Positions of the Nodes

North Node in the 1st House – South Node in the 7th House

In the past you may have always relied on others, and even moulded yourself around the expectations of others. This means that you may never have discovered your true individuality. In this lifetime, you need to step into a sense of independence, going it alone without needing the approval of others. Your identity may even have been submerged by others, so you have lost a sense of who you are.

Through self-starting actions, you can discover a deeper sense of self, your own true nature. You can still have relationships in your life, but they will be more balanced, in that you will be bringing all of yourself into the relationship, rather than a compromised version of you. It's important that both sides of the 1st/7th house axis here are recognised, so that the submissive side of the South Node does not dominate, nor the North Node in the 1st house become too overbearing.

Nevertheless, through taking independent action, you also start to develop a sense of strong will, and realise that you don't have to depend on others for your actions or their approval. You are your own person, perhaps even a natural leader, who can bring so much more back to a relationship. You are no longer dependent, but independent, and therefore all relationships can now be healthier. You need to develop in some parts of your life the courage to 'go it alone'. Initially this may feel uncomfortable – it is virgin territory where you need courage – but this is the way of your North Node, and where your treasure lies. You can even be a pioneer in what you do.

North Node in the 2nd house – South Node in the 8th

You may bring into this life a sense of emotional intensity, that you have secrets that need to be hidden. Even if this is not the case, you may be instinctively very private and secretive. There may be strong emotions of jealousy and possessiveness, and a strong pull towards sexual relationships. The South Node in the 8th can even indicate lifetimes where you experienced emotional crises and even mixed with the underworld, or were involved in crime. However, much more positively it can suggest deep spiritual understanding, and natural healing ability.

The North Node in the 2nd house encourages you to move towards a more stable, steady, even state emotionally, with less intensity. There can be a contentment and ease here, not wanting to be rushed or have sudden change imposed upon you. Your direction of soul travel is to develop calm in a crisis, so you need to lose the emotional crisis-prone emotions from the past.

The focus in this life is to build your own set of clear values, and also to have a sense of strong security. This can be financial and material security, as you may well have a natural business sense. You may be self-employed, which is common with the North Node in the 2nd, as it is to do with material self-sufficiency, so you don't have to rely on others. It is important to be financially self-sufficient, or at least move towards that. This material security can give you a solid base so you feel stable emotionally too; you don't have to experience the intense swings in feelings that you may have in the past.

This can also be a very creative position for your North Node. It is naturally linked to Taurus, the 2nd sign, known for its 'green thumb' cultivation abilities. This fertility in your nature can be good not only literally for growing things, but for building businesses too, based on your own clear values. The sign of the North Node will give you more information as to how these values should be expressed in the world. You can weave the spiritual knowledge from the past in all that you do.

North Node in the 3rd House – South Node in the 9th House

In the past you may have had much freedom to roam in foreign parts, and think big philosophical thoughts. You are a roamer, physically and mentally, an adventurer, and love to develop wisdom and study the interconnectedness of the universe. Meaning is a vital component to your beliefs, and although you have a broad range of understanding, you may never have stopped long enough to commit it to paper, to make it useful to others. Freedom and restless exploration were too important. You may have had a position of some authority in the past, and still feel that sense of confidence and presence in this life.

However, with the North Node in the 3rd house, this is the time to take action. You can't keep roaming like a gypsy and developing wonderful theories if they are not being brought down to people here and now to be useful. So now it's very important to put pen to paper, to write, blog, teach, publish, communicate in whatever way feels comfortable to you, to make coherent all the knowledge you already have within you. Remember it's always a weaving of the benefits of the South Node with that of the North, and in this case it is metaphysical knowledge or higher consciousness subjects. The sign of your North Node will show what you will be preoccupied with, and how you will communicate it.

There is also a sense of making it accessible and practical. This 3rd house has the sense of 'lower mind' while the 9th house is typically wisdom and 'higher mind'. However, higher mind is no use if it is not made accessible. An important part of the task of a 3rd house North Node is to turn this wisdom and knowledge into practical bite-sized pieces of information, so it is digestible and useful. The information becomes a coherent body of information, and ideally needs to be communicated simply and frequently to people, so everyone can understand. Social media today is a perfect vehicle for that, but writing and speaking of all kinds are valuable. This is the natural position of the teacher, stirring curiosity in others. It is about the dissemination of knowledge.

It is also the house area of the mentor, the counsellor and the advisor. Although the pull of the past in terms of roving and being a wild free spirit may still be strong, this lifetime is about at least communicating to the civilised world, even if you don't live in it yourself. You could develop quite a following with this Nodal position, as it is strongly linked to social media.

North Node in the 4th House – South Node in the 10th House

In the past you are likely to have held a high position of authority, and gained respect for your achievements. You probably had worked very hard to get to that position, and your reputation and status were important to you. You needed to be out in the world, building things, organising things, and working to make big long-term projects happen. You received much admiration for those achievements, and you may even have a slight superiority complex as you did so well.

Today, you may still wistfully yearn for those heady days of being out in the world and being recognised; but your task in this lifetime with this Nodal Axis is to focus on the home, the family, and giving emotional security rather than financial, although the home base itself will be important to you as security. You have to start to become aware of your emotions and feelings, and of those around you. The cosiness of home may seem too lowly and humble for you, and you may feel that you're not really 'achieving' anything, but the North Node in the 4th house requires a shift of values so that you see the importance of nurturing with your family and those you care for. It demands that you develop emotional depth yourself. If you keep trying to achieve in the world, and going towards your South Node, you may run into career difficulty, as your soul needs to grow towards your North Node.

This is quite a complex position for the Nodal Axis as it can suggest that one parent was more dominating than the other, and may have had high expectations of you; there may not have been enough space for emotion when you were young, which is why it has to be cultivated now.

You'll also need to understand the value of your family heritage and roots; but so often the value of this position is just being there and supporting others who need your understanding and care. It may also suggest that you increasingly are in a position where you have to care for others in some capacity, whether it is children or older people. The 'gold' of this North Node position is for others to feel emotionally sustained, and for you to recognise the value of something as humble as emotion, without having a title attached. Your past, however, will give you confidence in your role as protector. Just learn to be, and live, being aware of your feelings and all the value and richness they offer.

North Node in the 5th House – South Node in the 11th House

In the past you may have been idealistic and intellectual, but operating outside society because of your interests and ideas. You may have been an innovator, a scientist, or someone who cared deeply about the fate of others, a true humanitarian. You would have easily put any personal needs to one side, and submerged your identity with that of the group (whichever group was aligned with your ideals). You could well have been a visionary, very future-oriented, but driven principally by intellect and ideas. You may well have achieved something quite significant for the world.

There is still a pull now towards those lofty ideals, that any time focused on 'self' is an indulgence. However, this is where your pot of gold lies in this lifetime. This life's focus is about living from the heart rather than the head, but living with greater joy, spontaneity, fun, play and most importantly, creativity. You need to let your light shine and glory in that fully. Your greatest creations may be your children. You are likely to have great pride in them, and also enjoy a lot of playtime with them. Although there may still be a pull towards high ideals, it's important that you replace any intellectual detachment with a full embracement of life. A 5th house North Node needs to live life with enthusiasm, energy, radiance and generosity. This North Node position encourages you to live in the moment, and fill a room with joy. You need to develop uplifting energy for others, and natural leadership.

So rather than living on the periphery of society, where you have been with your 11th house South Node, you need to go towards the centre of life, even if that means participating in the mainstream. Unless other aspects in your birthchart contradict this, you may be happy being centre stage, especially if it involves your creativity. You should develop a natural flair and style too. You need to live fully from your heart energy in an open way, and have an instinctive generosity towards others. There's a love of life with this placement, of leaning forward into life rather than pulling away from it.

There's something else I've noticed with this South Node position. The 11th house is the house of lovability, how lovable you feel, and people with this placement often have a disproportionate need for the love and acceptance of others. This can dominate their behaviour, needing to be a 'people pleaser'. However, confidence and self-love will come via expressing the natural creativity of their North Node in the 5th house.

Although the habits of the past may still pull you back at times towards intellectualism and the betterment of society, your purpose in this life is to plunge fully into your individuality, celebrate your creativity, and love all that pass your way, especially children. You need to be present in the flow of life rather than anticipating the future and how it can be improved. You may even have a love of luxury and indulgence, savouring all the pleasures life has to offer, which you would not have allowed yourself in the past with your South Node in the 11th. Enjoyment figures high on your values; this is a fun-seeking North Node position. One of the main benefits that you will be bringing to the world is lifting the hearts of those around you, broadcasting both love and fun. However, your deeper purpose here is the integration of your South and North Node so you may actually help humankind in your own distinctive, unique way, through the innovation of your South Node and the creativity of your North Node.

North Node in the 6th House – South Node in the 12th House

In the past you may have been through a period of seclusion, whether voluntary or enforced. You may have experienced time in prisons or mental institutions, or more happily in retreats or communities where you were cut off from the mainstream world. You may have even experimented with drink, drugs or other addictive substances, and as a result of some or all of these experiences there was a dissolution of ego. The 12th house South Node symbolises withdrawal from the world, and in the natural horoscope is associated with the sign of Pisces.

This 12th house is that of the mystic, the seer, the healer, the visionary, who has dissolved ego to return to Source, and live in the flow of oneness and All That Is. There is a deep empathy with all beings, and a sensitivity to suffering. You may still have that profound sense of the divine intelligence of the cosmos, pervading all of life, and see the universe as one holistic whole. You may have strong psychic and intuitive skills, and perhaps be able to see and feel energy, and work with energy healing to help people.

The 12th house South Node can make you want to avoid commitment, and swim through the net and avoid anything that would pin you down too much day to day. Therefore there can be a tendency towards dreaming, drifting, fantasy, and not necessarily achieving anything tangible. You are more concerned with just being, and being in the flow of life, without any ambition or goals in any material sense. This pull back to Source is very seductive and beguiling, as it can make you want to avoid work or responsibility of any kind. However, with the North Node in the 6th house, in this incarnation that is precisely what is demanded.

Both the 12th and 6th house share a sense of humility and little ego, but the 6th house focus is much more grounded. Both ends of this Nodal Axis are prone to fretting and needless anxiety, but the more you focus on your work the less of an issue this will be. So you need to develop a strong work ethic, and be very focused and precise in the work you do, despite the pull back to the unfocused, dreamy way of being. Now this incarnation is a time of dedicated practical useful service to others. There is often an interest in diet and nutrition, and healing in general, particularly of the natural/alternative kind. As the 6th house is naturally aligned with the Earth sign of Virgo (6th sign), there is a sense here of using substances naturally found in and on the Earth to heal others. These can be herbs, essential oils, grounding/earthing where people physically connect to the Earth for healing, as well as homeopathy and other natural medicines. Energy and bodywork in general fall into the 6th house area too. There is a desire to make the body work efficiently, to clear blockages and impediments to good health, and the focus of the work can be very detailed and specific.

A wonderful combination of the 12th house South Node and 6th house North Node is to take the imagination, sensitivity and spiritual perception of the 12th house past, and weave that into a modality of practical service for others, particularly in the health and healing arena. You must develop a strong work ethic, commitment to your goals and a sense of responsibility. When using this 6th house energy well, you can become a workhorse, devoted to the care of others. There is a sense in this 6th house North Node of 'how can I help you in a practical way?' This can also include helping to care for animals, which is very connected to this 6th/12th house axis. The 6th house is linked to smaller animals, such as cats and dogs, the 12th house to larger animals such as horses. There can be an instinctive feeling and even communication with animals.

You may still wish to enjoy the stillness and meditation practice that may have been part of your 12th house South Node past; it will be helpful to still have a daily time of withdrawal from the world. Your dreams may still be vivid and insightful. You can gain much inspiration from this more ethereal past, but then bring it down to the world to be of practical use to others. It is vital with this Nodal Axis that your work in the world is meaningful to you, as this will drive your sense of purpose and alleviate any sense of victimhood from the past. Work may well become a principal focus in this lifetime.

North Node in the 7th House – South Node in the 1st House

In the past you may have achieved a great deal in terms of independence and solo, pioneering action. You still have a sense of strong willpower and focus, and are used to a high level of freedom and 'going it alone'. In fact, you wouldn't really think too much of how courageous this has been, as the South Node in the 1st house echoes the South Node in Aries. It is a simple, direct instinct of 'I want to do that; I will go and do it now'. Therefore your personal achievements may have been great, and you may not have even noticed that you were flying solo much of the time. In this incarnation, you may still carry much restlessness and desire for freedom, and not necessarily want to have to consider others' feelings or needs in your life. You may have had the respect and admiration of others in all that you conquered in your life.

However, with the North Node in the 7th house, your task in this lifetime is to bring others into your picture. You are no longer supposed to go it alone, for the purposes of your soul growth, but to work in relationships and collaborations for a better result. You may have a tendency that may be considered selfish to just go and do things without consulting others; this time around it is vital that you take their views into consideration, otherwise life will not work very well. You are likely to hit many relationship hurdles until you have learned this different focus, and no longer operate as a loner. Whenever you follow independent behaviour, your life may not work so well, as you are falling back on your South Node house position.

It is important for relationships of all kinds to be the focus in this life. You are here to develop kindness, consideration, understanding, and become more 'other-directed' in your behaviour. The gifts of diplomacy and balance are key here, as well as compromise. You cannot simply dash off to do something you urgently want to do, without consulting others. In the past you were developing your Mars characteristics, the male principle and in myth the god of war (Mars rules Aries and therefore naturally the first house). There is a sense of the warrior, the pioneer, the one who has battled against great odds. In this lifetime you must develop the antidote to that brashness and selfishness, and use your Venus (natural ruler of the 7th house) which represents love, harmony, consideration and co-operation. When you use this 7th house North Node, you will see that not only will life flow much more easily, but the results from collaboration will be so much better. You may work with, or be supported by, a romantic partner, but the 7th house also represents your relationship with the public too, and the importance of that in this life.

Balance is key with this Nodal Axis; focus on others with an open heart, but keep the clear sense of self that you have developed from the past. The benefit of your South Node in the 1st house will always give you the courage and sureness of self you need in any situation in life, but it must be tempered from a 'me-first' attitude to one of 'we'. Even if you feel the restless pull of solo achievement, it is better to give that strength and willpower that you have built up in the past to others, rather than glory in it yourself. You will gradually start to see how uplifting and satisfying this is to help others in this way. You must feel no resentment in doing this, as that is still feeding your South Node tendencies rather than your North Node.

So this lifetime is all about being focused on others and their needs, and doing it with kindness and grace. It is about keeping the balance between a healthy sense of self, but without any dominating ego. You must release wilfulness and learn compromise. The sign of the North Node will shed light on how you can best express this in your life.

North Node in the 8th House – South Node in the 2nd House

You are here to learn about power, in its different forms. In the past you may have developed good business acumen, or conversely there may have been issues around money. Either way, it is likely that you developed a strong acquisitive attitude, tightly possessing all that you owned. There can be a scarcity philosophy here, so whatever you gain you hold very tightly, in case it is lost. Material possessions and money matter a great deal to you, and help you to define who you are. You may love good food and wine, the good things in life, the sensual pleasures and comforts, with your home having beautiful fabrics and items of value. Value to you comes in a tangible, material form, and you are not aware of other people's values, which may be very different to yours.

Your emotions may still be intense too; feelings of jealousy, possessiveness, and strong sexuality may still dominate your emotional nature. Your desire to accumulate may include people with whom you are in a relationship; this is the legacy of the past. Feelings with this South Node position can be quite fixed; there can be a real reluctance to be flexible and open to change. However, the North Node in the 8th house goes beyond change, to transformation. You are here partly to understand energy exchange, and the power of that.

You may still have feelings of stubbornness and even laziness from the past, that you want life to be easy and comfortable. There needs to be a complete reorientation of values with this Nodal Axis. An 8th house North Node requires a shift from a focus on your own values and possessions to those of others. Indeed, holding onto possessions is likely to become deadening for you, so your attention needs to move from things to much deeper values around spiritual knowledge and understanding. You need to develop an interest in the 'underside' of life, how reality works, and most importantly how you can transform your nature.

You may still have emotional intensity, but need to lose the fixity of the 2nd house South Node (which is naturally associated with the sign of Taurus). The 8th house North Node has the natural sign association with Scorpio. This has an ancient ruler of Mars, planet of energy, assertion and goals, and a modern ruler of Pluto, planet of transformation. Therefore your North Node has a greater sense of movement forward, of propulsion, rather than fiercely guarding the status quo. It offers a deeper sense of connection, intimacy, and trust with others. Rather than the defence of your 2nd house South Node, there is a greater feeling of focus and purpose. You need to shed all the old attitudes from the past of possessiveness, materialism and a constant defence of the status quo, to being open to a deeper relationship with the world. You may even experience some financial loss (2nd house South Node = money) in order to accelerate your growth towards your North Node in the 8th house.

At one level, this required shift in perspective from your own values to other people's can mean that you work in an area connected to other people's money (their material values). It is very common to see an 8th house North Node working in insurance, investments or banking in some capacity. However, the deeper shift from 2nd house South Node to the 8th house North Node is a shift from material values to spiritual values. The need is to develop a fascination for the deeper motivations of others, a forensic mind that wants to get to the bottom of things, particularly concerning the nature of life and our mortality. There can be a deep interest in reincarnation. This North Node position can also be excellent for research, and for working as a consultant for others. There can be an interest in the nature of power, and different forms of power, be they financial, emotional, psychological, sexual or spiritual. This 8th house North Node can be quite ruthless with self in achieving a depth of being that is a very long way from where you entered life with the South Node in the 2nd house. The sign position of the 8th house North Node will give you some clues as to where this transformation needs to operate in your life.

Another way that the 8th house North Node can manifest is in the area of alternative healing; I am seeing this more and more in clients' lives as an expression of the spiritual side of this North Node placement.

North Node in the 9th house – South Node in the 3rd House

In the past you had a curious mind, and you may still retain that curiosity today. You may have had linguistic ability, and the mind worked by osmosis, able to pick up information and knowledge all the time, from anything you read or observed. Therefore you have gathered a great deal of information, but it may have breadth but no depth. The South Node energy here may be scattered, pieces of data all of which are interesting but form no coherence. Your mind is sharp, and may be witty. You are likely still to have acute powers of observation, and be a very social animal, always involved in other people's lives. Siblings may have particular karmic significance with this Nodal Axis.

The South Node in the 3rd house symbolises 'lower mind', the chatter of day-to-day conversations and observations, which can act as distractions and make you indecisive. The purpose of your 9th house North Node is to move you to 'higher mind' wisdom. To move from the scattered chatter of the past, and to start to envisage the meaning behind this information, and see a bigger picture, bigger horizons, in terms of the interconnectedness of the universe. You need to develop an interest in how reality works in the metaphysical world in order to fulfil this North Node position. This is a Nodal Axis that must move closer to a definition of 'God', however you define that.

You may be drawn to travel to distant places, but the point of the travel is not just to lie on a beach but to better understand other cultures, and the meaning that they have in their belief systems. You have to leave home behind. Or you may simply be a traveller with the mind, exploring ideas, philosophies, big visions, and be a gypsy, a roamer, an explorer. You need to become a natural philosopher and visionary, with strong intuition and almost an ability to see into the future; always underpinned by meaning, this becomes your own personal wisdom. There will be natural writing talent here, and speaking talent. You may be an inspired teacher, an author, a broadcaster of some kind, as both ends of this Nodal Axis are about communication in its various forms.

It will be important to you to have the freedom to explore your thinking in deeper ways. You need to work on developing a coherent belief system or philosophy that takes all the scattered knowledge from the past but puts it into an organised form. Only then does it really have value. You may feel pulled back at times to trivia and a busy social life, and feel how easy it was to be socially adept with people, but this lifetime may be a little more isolated; however, it is offering you a deeper sense of being. Your purpose with the North Node in the 9th, ironically, is to think about purpose in a general way for us all. What is the meaning of being here on Earth? How does the cosmos fit together, and what does that understanding mean for us as humankind? You need to be a free, roaming thinker, a 'questor', and living in civilisation becomes less important. You may even have a draw towards big horizons and wild instinctive places in nature. You ideally need to live with a big horizon to become a big thinker. There is a need to broaden the mind; you should develop a fascination for the 'truth' as you see it, having explored many truths.

The North Node in the 9th house should encourage you to write, teach, explore abstract subjects such as philosophy, and possibly religion. You may have had sporting talent when young, but increasingly are now drawn to active spiritual practices such as yoga, t'ai chi and qigong.

In the past you may have dedicated yourself completely to your family and their emotional needs; you may have been embroiled in all their feelings and issues, and your focus was based around the home. You may always instinctively want to stay home, or conversely it may feel like a prison; it can feel suffocating. Now, with the North Node in the 10th house, you must step out and develop in the world.

This will involve a lot of hard work, and you will need to show integrity at every step. This will be important in building a solid reputation and status, and you have the potential to achieve a great deal in the world, and become someone of authority. It may feel like a shift between the more feminine, gentle part of yourself that was involved with the family in the past, and the masculine need to define yourself out in the world now. Sometimes this may feel like a struggle, that you feel pulled back to the emotional needs of the family; being back in the family nest may give you the support you need too. However, this life is meant to be less 'cosy' than the past; it involves deliberately stepping out into the world to provide the financial security for the family, rather than the emotional security. There may be still some entanglements from the past in that you still need to deal with family issues to some extent, and may even find yourself playing both traditional roles of mother (emotional support) and father (financial support) to the family. That can mean at times you feel pulled both ways, or that the demands are heavy; but the potential for achievement in this lifetime is great.

Your North Node in the 10th house should encourage your ambition, make you want to build something that you can point to, and feel that you achieved that. It is often a steady, persistent climb to the top, respecting other authority figures along the way and being able to work with, or for, big institutions. Generally this North Node position can be quite conventional in its orientation (unless it is in the sign of Aquarius, the maverick). You need to develop a sense of responsibility, and your organisational abilities are likely to be excellent. The Nodal Axis gives the potential for real leadership in the world in some capacity, and the sign on the cusp of the 10th house gives more information as to how that will be achieved.

The North Node in the 10th house should give you a feeling of purpose and meaning that go beyond the family. There is a greater feeling of 'going it alone' than you may have had in the past when you were in the midst of family support. There is more self-definition here, and it is very important that you try to move away from any feelings of nostalgia, moodiness or sentimentality, and don't sink back into the past. The South Node in the 4th house can suggest co-dependent relationships, whereas the North Node in the 10th can encourage you to carve out your own destiny in the world. It is brave, ambitious and respected, and more a sense of building a future yourself, while still having the support of your family in the background.

North Node in the 11th House – South Node in the 5th House

In the past you may have delighted in love affairs, having fun and a life of pleasure. It was very focused around your ego and individual creative talents, and you were recognised and applauded for those. There may have been an element of the *puer aeternus*, the eternal youth, where you didn't have to take much responsibility, but lived a life of pleasure, joy and romantic adventures. Life was very much about celebrating the self. The 5th house in the natural zodiac is the sign of Leo, so this is where the individual naturally shines their light to the world, as long as it is reflected back to them too.

Now, there is a need to leave that ego focus behind, and be concerned with the more serious business of the needs of the collective and society. As your North Node is in the 11th house, you need to develop a sense of idealism around the collective, ensure that you are focused in an intellectual way on improving the 'common good of all', however you decide to express that. So ego should be put to one side as you submerge your efforts into the group that you become associated with. At times you may hanker for the past in terms of ego recognition – 'what about me?' – but the evolution of your soul demands that this becomes secondary to improving the world in some way. You may still yearn to be loved in a deep personal way (South Node in the 5th house), and this continues with your 11th house North Node; but this time around what you seek is more of an appreciation and admiration for your ideas and your innovation. It reflects the 'head' of the 11th house North Node position, versus the 'heart' of the 5th house South Node.

There is often a sense of operating outside society, or espousing interests that are not yet mainstream, as you can be ahead of your time. You may have interest in scientific or alternative subjects that society generally rejects or is unaware of as yet. So you are championing issues which will improve society in the future. This may be anything from helping your neighbours in unusual ways, to joining global humanitarian organisations. The urge is for a better world, and that is the virgin territory towards which you must head. You can be a visionary for the future.

Part of you may still want to have more fun, take time off to play, and be indulgent; but your greater sense of idealism should drive you on to achieve more in your life than that. This lifetime isn't just about you; it's about the collective, and your ideals. One of the benefits of the North Node in the 11th house is that you are likely to develop a strong social network and set of friendships, people of like mind that you may consider to be your 'tribe'. You can become a great networker with this position, acting as a connector between people to be of mutual benefit. You can also use the creativity that you have developed with your South Node in the 5th house to promote and express whatever you are working on within the collective.

This offers a quirky, unusual potential for new ideas to be developed: you have the potential to be an innovator, and achieve something unique for mankind.

North Node in the 12th House – South Node in the 6th House

In the past you may have been very detail-oriented, compartmentalising and analysing everything. There is likely to have been a streak of perfectionism with this, even towards yourself, so if you didn't do everything absolutely perfectly then you were your own worst self-critic. The South Node in the 6th house is aligned with Virgo (as this is the 6th sign), the worrywart. So you may have been someone who was always anxious and restless, questioning your own abilities and often being full of self-doubt.

You may still carry these feelings with you in this life, never feeling good enough, and having perhaps even some bitterness or jealousy towards other people. In the past you may have had a focus on health, and it's important not to let your mental attitude affect your physical well-being. In this life, with the North Node in the 12th house, you are being asked to develop a divergent outlook rather than a convergent. So there is a need to move from analysis and worrying towards love and surrender. Just relax, release and let go, and trust in divine intelligence. Release all the worry to whatever or whomever you perceive as God, or your higher self.

The South Node in the 6th house suggests that in the past you were concerned with defining boundaries to things, identifying them and pinning them down to be specific; now with the North Node in the 12th, none of that matters. Just surrender, 'let go and let God'. Both ends of this Nodal Axis share a sense of humility, little ego, and also a need for service. The South Node in the 6th house is concerned with practical service, whereas the North Node in the 12th is concerned with spiritual service. This involves developing compassion, empathy, love, and being concerned about the collective and their consciousness. You need to work in some way with dreams, depth psychology, healing, behind the scenes charity or caring work, perhaps even being involved with the dying. It will be very helpful to you to be drawn to these areas, but also to find time to withdraw, retreat, pull back from the daily fretting worries of the world and just dissolve into a state of oneness with the universe. You can do this through meditation, listening to music, breath work, being in nature, candle gazing, or whatever means you are drawn to, to achieve this state of bliss and dissolution.

Part of the North Node in the 12th house may also be to develop your creative ability. This sense of oneness, or 'touching the divine', will bring you some of the inspiration for this. You will fully be living your North Node in the 12th when you can live more and more in this state of universal bliss, while feeling you are being of spiritual service to others. This is one of the most important positions for soul growth in this lifetime. It is about serving the collective.

The 12th house North Node is often drawn to working with animals, particularly large animals such as horses. The work is likely to be of a healing nature, or the ability to communicate with animals instinctively and almost telepathically. This is a 'tuning-in' ability, a fine perception that enables the healing to take place.

Now be sure to fill in the part of the worksheet that covers your:

- **North Node sign**
- **North Node house**
- **North Node planetary ruler (planet ruling the sign that your NN is in)**
- **North Node planetary ruler's house**
- **South Node sign**
- **South Node house**

Write down any other ideas that come to you around ways that you may already be, or you would wish to be, expressing your Nodal Axis in your life. Write down as many meanings as you can of your Nodal Axis as outlined above. Are you still falling back towards your South Node, or making progress towards your North Node? Imagine that you are painting a canvas, and each piece of information is an important component of your final painting.

If you are confident of other elements of your chart, such as your Ascendant, your Sun or Moon, or any area of your chart where you have three or more planets, please add those into your worksheet.

You have now learned a lot about yourself since you started this book, but the next brushstroke on the canvas for you is to consider your **Midheaven sign**. This may be one of the main ways you will be expressing your Nodal Axis to the world, as it is linked to your life path too, and career.

What does your Midheaven say?

Your Midheaven in your birthchart is where the Sun was at its highest point overhead at the time of your birth. In your birthchart this can be marked at the top of the chart by 'MC' (Medium Coeli) or 'Midheaven', or just a stronger black line or arrow pointing upwards, somewhere around the 12 o'clock position of your birthchart. If it isn't particularly marked, then use the 10th house cusp, which will be your Midheaven. The Midheaven is shown clearly on birthcharts downloaded from my website.

Why is this important? The Midheaven is often an important part of how you will be expressing your Nodal Axis in the world, as the sign of the Midheaven represents how we would like to be seen by others. It's a large part of how we manifest our soul's journey. It represents our career, and the Midheaven sign also suggests the kind of work we are normally drawn to, but most importantly the *approach* we have to our work, and the qualities and values we would like to express through it. It can also represent how we would like to be remembered in our contribution to the world. This is going to be important in defining your life path.

For instance, my own Midheaven is in Virgo. This is one of the signs ruled by Mercury, and therefore Virgo can be linked to communication, which has been the entire theme of my career in its various forms. My Midheaven and its ruler Mercury define my work, whether it is writing, speaking, blogging, or broadcasting via YouTube and my newsletters; I have a strong urge to communicate with people. Interestingly, as Virgo is linked to the intestines and digestive system, people with a Virgo Midheaven are often involved in dietary advice; when I was young I considered becoming a nutritionist, and still have a great interest in diet and nutrition. However, with the focus of my North Node in the 3rd house of communication, the balance was tilted in my career towards that, rather than nutrition.

It is so fascinating to look back at these decisions, even before I knew anything about astrology, in terms of how these nudges and urges of the soul were playing a part in my life direction.

However, considering the approach I take to my work, it has always been one of wanting to be of service to others, in a practical way (Virgo is an Earth sign). I tend to be very work-focused, as anyone with Virgo emphasis can have workaholic tendencies, and I try to be very thorough and perfectionist in whatever I do. I don't take shortcuts or do anything in a sloppy way; everything has to be thoroughly prepared and organised so I can give the most to my clients in their consultations. I strongly recognise this Virgo element in all my work. It can help to give humility too: it is all about the work, not the person.

So now we are going to go through the descriptions of the Midheaven through all 12 signs, for this is one of the important ingredients to focus on in co-creating your life. You only need to read the description which is relevant to your birthchart. It's important to say that these descriptions may seem very practical, but try and see them in the bigger context of your soul purpose this time around. Again, the alchemy has to come from you in going beyond these descriptions and envisaging how you can live them out in your life.

Midheaven in Aries – ruled by Mars

Ruled by Mars, Aries is one of the most ambitious placements for your Midheaven. It suggests a strong drive and focus to achieve, and you would have natural leadership qualities. You are not only happy to take the lead, but also to go solo, and be a pioneer in your work. There is admiration for strength, courage and assertiveness in work, taking tough decisions, and an ability to work quickly and be decisive. Generally there is energy and great focus demonstrated in the work, and high achievement is very important. This may (depending on the rest of the chart) take the form of sporting achievement, especially in early life, as Aries is a very physical, driving, active fire sign. There is often impatience to achieve, wanting to get things moving quickly, and potentially this is a great placement for 'troubleshooters': people who can come in and shake up any staleness to achieve a more streamlined operation. An Aries Midheaven is very common in the charts of entrepreneurs and solo workers, who want to do it their way, and quickly.

Midheaven in Taurus – ruled by Venus

Ruled by Venus, this suggests that your career will be involved with beauty or things of value in some way. Depending on the rest of the chart, this could be with people, homes or beautiful possessions such as jewellery or antiques. Taurus has an affinity for beautiful shiny things of value. It also manifests as a love for beautiful fabrics, textures and colours.

It is important that the work environment is beautiful, peaceful, and that it has a state of harmony and a sense of nurturing.

Other expressions of a Midheaven in Taurus, as it is a fixed Earth sign, is to work with the Earth, making beautiful gardens, or to be involved in farming or sustainability. The rest of the chart will give clues as to which way this will go, but there is a fertility around Taurus, a desire to make things grow and be lovely. Sometimes Taurus Midheaven is found working with land or real estate, or building, because of its connection to the Earth and enduring tangible things of value.

As Taurus has this strong sense of value, it is one of the most common Midheaven signs involved with banking and wealth management.

Another expression of a Taurus Midheaven is for you to work with the physical body, for example as an aromatherapist, giving massage or doing energy work. There is a strong tactile sense with Taurus, so working with the body is a natural way to help people via a sense of touch.

Unlike Aries, Taurus likes to approach things slowly, steadily, and with a strongly developed appreciation of the physical senses. There is no rush; it is important to feel grounded. There is often very good business judgement with Taurus Midheaven, because of this grounded sense. Decisions (unless the chart has indicators to the contrary) are usually taken slowly and carefully.

Midheaven in Gemini – ruled by Mercury

Ruled by Mercury, a Midheaven in Gemini is very connected to communication. There is normally a dexterity with communication, and you are usually articulate, witty and observant, and often linguistically talented. You want to be seen as quick and intelligent. Writing, journalism, teaching and translating all come to the fore in the work area, as well as selling, media and telecommunications, administration and secretarial/PA work. Another area for the career is navigation, working with maps, and (taxi) driving. Gemini is connected with short journeys, coming and going, hence these links. Another area which is common is the merchant, the trader, the importer/exporter. These are all linked to rapid exchange, and linked to day-to-day life, which has associations with Mercury and Gemini.

Those with a Gemini Midheaven are often seen as 'mercurial'; they seem quick to understand, curious and bright. There is a mental lightness and flexibility to them, and are the sign most easily able to multi-task; hence, they frequently have two careers in their lives, sometimes running simultaneously.

Midheaven in Cancer – ruled by the Moon

Ruled by the Moon, Cancer is the sign most associated with nurturing. Therefore common careers are catering and cooking, literally nourishing people; or it can be expressed as an emotional nurturing, so they can work as carers, or people involved in the caring professions.

Cancer is the sign most associated with motherhood, so it is common to see people following a career of child-minder, teacher (usually of younger ages), or even surrogate mother. Usually there is a need to express loving, caring emotion in the career.

However, as Cancer is also linked to the home, this can manifest as helping people find homes, often safe and secure homes where this has been lacking in the past.

Midheaven in Leo – ruled by the Sun

Ruled by the Sun, a Midheaven in Leo indicates someone whose identity is tied in with their work. They need to 'shine', be seen as someone special, and recognised, admired and applauded. This can be an ambitious placement, and if a wife has not achieved this for herself it may be important to live this energy out via a successful husband.

The individual with a Leo Midheaven wants to be seen as powerful, authoritative and strong, and often runs his/her own business. They want to be seen as the 'king' in what they do. There is a dramatic and often flamboyant flair and style with Leo, so they are sometimes involved in performing arts, acting or fashion, any career that demands individual style being offered as a service, and luxury goods. The career offering can be linked to prestige and status. Leo has a love for the good life.

You would want the freedom to express creatively and dramatically in your work, and most likely (depending on the rest of your birthchart), be centre stage in what you are doing.

Midheaven in Virgo – ruled by Mercury

The sign of Virgo is also ruled by Mercury, as is Gemini, so there is a clear link here to the world of communication in all its forms. Virgo has a strong discriminatory sense, so with its excellent logic and organising ability, it can bring order out of chaos. This lends itself to many administrative and organisational positions, but Virgo is particularly good at detail. Therefore careers demanding a very detailed eye and a love of detail are common, such as accountancy. As Virgo has a highly critical sense, you may work as a literary critic or editor.

There is a sense of wanting to be of practical service to others, and this can take many forms. Mercury always has a day-to-day connection, so an individual with Virgo Midheaven may offer services such as space-clearing, feng shui, time management, PA work, or organising your life in a more efficient way. Virgo is the sign most linked to efficiency. It has more of a practical bias than an intellectual one: what can I do to help people, day to day?

The other common manifestation as I mentioned with my own birthchart is that because Virgo rules the intestinal and digestive areas, people are often involved in nutrition and diet. There can be a fascination for making the body, and particularly the digestion, work more efficiently. Virgo is linked to purification, so detoxing can be part of the offering.

Virgo also has links to health and hygiene in a more general way, and it is one of the most common Midheaven positions for people working in the medical area, making sure everything connected to the body is clean, healthy, hygienic and efficient.

Midheaven in Libra – ruled by Venus

Libra, like Taurus, is ruled by Venus, so the same importance around beauty would apply. A Libra Midheaven is common in the fashion business, as there is an elegance and style here, in a more conventional way than some of the other signs. It can be linked to the arts and cultural worlds, and to entertainment in general. People with this aspect like to be recognised for their grace, style and taste.

Libra is the sign of the 'go-between', so it is common in people who work in PR, the diplomatic service, with lawyers and mediators, and even politicians, translating what one party wants and balancing that with what the other party wants too. Along with a Sagittarius Midheaven, these two signs are the most common in lawyers or anyone connected with the law. Libra brings in a strong sense of fairness and justice into whatever the work is. Any form of consulting may have a Libran Midheaven, and you very often work with a partner in your career, either a business partner or a spouse. Libra is so 'other-directed' that there is a need to share ideas, and see how the other person responds before taking them out to the world.

There is usually a lot of charm and diplomacy in this situation, and it is an excellent Midheaven for anyone who wants to bring more beauty, balance and peace into the world.

Where the rest of the chart supports this, I've commonly seen a Libran Midheaven operate as the 'go-between' when the person is a medium, or very psychic, with a foot in each world.

Midheaven in Scorpio – ruled by Pluto

This is usually an ambitious placement, as Scorpio is ruled by Pluto, which has terrific focus and drive. There is a 'digging deep' quality with Scorpio, wanting to get to the bottom of things, so you would be excellent at any kind of research or forensic work, and it is common in the charts of people involved in the mining industry – literally digging deep. Scorpio Midheaven people tend to approach their careers with great intensity, and their work has to be engaging and deeply meaningful to them.

Common careers are psychology, medicine (getting to the bottom of the problem), radiotherapy (the Pluto connection), and investigative journalism. Sometimes the work may have a secret element to it, and it can also be where you may be involved in helping people in the 'underworld' in some way; people who are criminal, or have been involved in underhand activity, or have felt sidelined by society. A Scorpio Midheaven would understand these primal emotions well, and often wants to transform (Pluto) that person's life.

This regenerative side of Scorpio can also apply to other things like furniture or homes, but there is more commonly an emotional component to the work. Satisfaction in the career is achieved by digging deep and rehabilitating people.

Scorpio is one of the most spiritual signs, so another dimension of how this Midheaven position can operate is in the spiritual/alternative healing area.

Midheaven in Sagittarius – ruled by Jupiter

Ruled by Jupiter, this mutable fire sign may have many possible careers. It is always important for you to have a good reputation, and bring a lot of energy, enthusiasm and insight to whatever you are doing. Status and recognition are vital too.

Sport is an obvious career, at least in the early life, as Sagittarius rules the thighs and athletics. Along with Libra, it is the most common Midheaven position in the charts of lawyers; or people involved in teaching, as the sign is excellent at provoking curiosity in others, and also education in a broader sense. In fact, any career which tries to bring a greater sense of vision to people's lives, as Sagittarius is future-oriented, and can bring a sense of inspiration and bigger and better possibilities to others. It is also strongly linked to inspirational writing and publishing, especially where there is a strong belief system that underpins this. It is also one of the signs linked to travel and internationalism, so travel may feature as an important part of your work, or at least lots of foreign contacts. It can manifest as international marketing and banking, though there has to be a sense of meaningfulness in the work; the sign is all about finding meaning in the career.

There is another side to Sagittarius which is connected to the instinctive, tribal, ancient side of life, with big horizons and a sense of connecting to something that we may have lost in modern life. It is a sense of ancient wisdom, which you may want to access in some way in your career. This may also link to a strong sense of idealism to which the sign is associated.

There always has to be enthusiasm, and the sense of 'bigger and better' in your career, fulfilling the restless energy of Sagittarius.

Midheaven in Capricorn – ruled by Saturn

Capricorn is ruled by Saturn. Therefore your position in your career is often achieved after much work and discipline. Capricorn is a very 'conventional' sign, and has outstanding organisational ability. It is said that those with this Midheaven could organise an army. Hence the areas of work are likely to include administration and organisation, and teaching. Capricorn is about top-down structures and power, so you can probably (depending on the rest of your birthchart) operate either in or for a big organisation, and may steadily work your way up to management status. In fact, status and reputation are likely to be important to you too; a sense of achievement is important, often in terms of a title or position.

A Capricorn Midheaven is also linked to a scientific career, as Saturn is about precision, often with a talent in mathematics. Saturn as a planet is linked to construction, so you may work as a builder or surveyor, but ultimately work your way up to be a manager of a building company.

Saturn is connected to a strong sense of morality, right and wrong, so you may be involved in work where the imposition of society's rules and morals is part of your job. There can be judgement of others with this, and it is therefore common in the charts of people who work as Justices of the Peace, or policemen, enforcing the rules and discipline of society.

Capricorn is a very conservative energy, so your work is likely to be something mainstream which is seen to be 'respectable' that would be approved of by society.

Midheaven in Aquarius – ruled by Uranus

Aquarius always likes to challenge the status quo and take a different line. It is the sign most associated with humanitarianism and egalitarianism, and therefore there is often an urge in your work to do something to 'help the common good', whether that is a neighbourhood or global effort. People with an Aquarius Midheaven don't normally feel that comfortable in a hierarchical structure; they feel more comfortable in a collective environment where everyone has an equal but different part to play; but it is important that you have freedom of self-expression, so you can express your individuality in your work, and don't have to suffer interference from others. Freedom and independence are very important.

It's important to be seen as unique, socially conscious, and bringing change, reform, innovation and even new inventions and new technology to the world. You don't want to be seen as ordinary, and there is always the hint of the rebel in your work. Often you can suddenly change (Uranus) careers. Sometimes the work is quirky and unusual, so you are exploring a 'niche' where your consumers may not be mainstream either. There is often an involvement in alternative subjects of all kinds: therapies, energy work, astrology, and anything that you feel expresses your pursuit of the 'truth'.

As Aquarius is highly innovative, and Uranus can have a scientific talent, sometimes this Midheaven position can produce new unusual scientific inventions. Aquarius is the sign of the inventor. It is also highly idealistic and quite future-oriented. Uranus has links to the superconscious, and there is often a sense of being 'wired' with ideas in your work. Electronics and anything connected with IT or computing are also expressions of an Aquarius Midheaven, as its ruler Uranus is linked to all things electrical. As Aquarius also links with the electrical energy of the body, I am seeing this more commonly in the charts of acupuncturists and vibrational healers.

Midheaven in Pisces – ruled by Neptune

Pisces is ruled by Neptune, and there are many likely career options with this placement. Firstly, Pisces is highly creative and artistic, so the work could focus around beauty, art, music, fashion, or some other creative outlet depending on the information from the rest of the chart. You may have a slightly dreamy or unfocused approach to work, so the creativity is unlikely to be with words, and is more usually focused around music, art or fashion.

Neptune is connected to a beautiful quality of light, so photography and film work may feature in the career. If you pursue the creative route, imagination will play a big part in whatever you do.

Linked to this, Neptune also has associations of glamour and illusion, and you may work in the television or film world. Pisces on the Midheaven is about 'going viral', and therefore people can become celebrities or very well known with this placement.

There is also a different career expression available to this Midheaven. Pisces has strong connections with healing, and therefore either the more orthodox career of medicine or nursing may come up, or it could be alternative healing. The urge is to serve here; there can be a feeling of sacrifice in whatever work you do, a sense of devotion, of putting aside 'egoic' needs to be of spiritual service to others.

If you have a Pisces Midheaven you can at times be very confused about what to do, as at a lower level it can manifest as discontent, disillusionment and lack of focus as to which work to pursue. At a higher level it is spiritual inspiration, and being of spiritual service to others.

Now fill in your worksheet with your:

- **Midheaven sign**
- **Midheaven sign's planetary ruler**
- **Are there any other ideas that have come to you as a result of understanding your Midheaven sign and ruler?**
- **Do they reflect the kind of work you have already been doing?**
- **How is it blending with your Nodal Axis in terms of expressing these in the world?**
- **Are there any commonalities or natural links?**
- **What is this stirring inside of you?**
- **Can you see how you may be able to express your Midheaven in a different or bigger way in your life?**

Write down as many meanings as you can for your Midheaven and its planetary ruler.

Nodal Axis in relationships

Just before we leave the Nodal Axis and go onto further discuss the ruler of your Midheaven, there is another important point that you may find interesting about your Nodes. Again and again, in important relationships I see very close contacts (conjunctions, but also squares and oppositions) between one person's Nodal Axis (either North or South Nodes) and the other person's Ascendant, Midheaven, Sun, Moon or Venus, or between the Nodal Axes of the pair. These connections are often the most powerful of any birthchart aspects between people, and these appear to act as a very strong attractor between people, however unlikely the outside packaging appears. They seem to provide an ancient glue, encouraging longevity in the relationship. There is often a sense of deep familiarity and unfathomability in this attraction, as if you have known each other before. The dance goes on.

Planet that rules the sign on your Midheaven

The last brushstroke on the canvas for the purposes of this book is the planet that rules the sign on your Midheaven. As I mentioned, my Midheaven is in Virgo, and Mercury rules that sign, so that is the planet that is important for me in my career (the planet of communication). Just refer to the Midheaven sign list above to discover which planet rules your Midheaven sign.

Just think about the symbolism of that planet, and what it adds to the picture for you.

Now we have the exciting part, which is about creating your future vision for your future self from these important elements of your chart. Just before that, I'd like to share some helpful daily context for this future you.

6 Daily Context

"It's never too late to be what you might have been."

George Eliot, Author

Before we start building the vision of your future self, I'd like to share some daily context thoughts that I've developed in my own life, to help you to manifest your future you.

One thing that I try to achieve consistently, whatever is happening in my life, is to be 'smile abundant'. Whenever I'm interacting with people, and even in my YouTube videos, I try to smile. Smiling is the most ancient method of non-verbal positive interaction with others, and tends to induce the same behaviour in others, known as 'mirroring'. So if I smile at people in my daily comings and goings in shops and stores, they are much more likely to smile back. So the smiles ripple out into the world, and certainly improve my daily reality.

More than that, it has been proven that the simple act of smiling releases endorphins, the happy chemicals, into your system, whether you have something to smile about or not. However, in that wonderful create-your-own-reality feedback loop, if it improves our body chemistry we are more likely to attract events that make us happy, so it's an all-round win.

In this turbulent world, try to develop a daily spiritual practice in which you feel you are connecting to Source, however you define this. This is a sense of knowing there is a cosmic divine intelligence which constantly supports your growth. We are all connected in this holistic universe. The more you can cultivate this feeling of connection, by definition the less you will feel separate, alone, and overwhelmed by whatever is happening in the world, and your world. Whether this spiritual practice is your own form of meditation, breath work, mindfulness, being in nature, or candle gazing, it becomes your default setting. It becomes so familiar that you can quickly and easily almost fall into this place, so that it becomes your spiritual anchor and compass. You develop a greater sense of calm and peace. You may start to feel a sense of timelessness and eternity. Your inner guidance system then becomes your navigator through life. Do certain events, people or situations make you feel heavy or light? Stressed or relaxed? Watch your body reaction to things through your day and try to structure your day so you have more of the happy, supportive people and events, rather than the stressful, anxious ones. Try to surround yourself with people on your wavelength, your frequency, rather than feeling you are compromising or being dragged down by those you spend time with. In fact, the more challenging things are in the outside world, the more we need to create our own energetic reality in this way.

When we develop a daily spiritual practice, we have a much stronger place from which to create our reality. Turbulent events may happen in the world, but they do not affect us so much. We are more likely to simply observe them, but not engage with negative emotions. We develop a sense of inner strength, knowing we can just sink back into our divine spark whenever we wish, so it becomes second nature for us. We are then much less likely to be buffeted by outer events, and much more in control of our own state of mind.

Another aspect of spiritual practice that I find helpful is to create a meditation space. This can be a place in your home that physically is always the place you meditate, as it starts to build up peaceful energy in that area. However, in addition I recommend creating a place in your mind that you always go to. This may be somewhere you know and have visited, such as a beautiful clearing in a forest, near a stream, perhaps. Or you can create from your imagination, seeing a deep cave with sparking quartz all around, and a crystal clear lake at the bottom where you can see your visions. It's whatever comes to mind as being right for you. This creates a feeling of familiarity and 'default', so that you can always just slip into that safe space that will undoubtedly take on a life of its own over time with your meditating energy. It helps to strengthen your daily practice, and give you a clearer sense of centre.

Then if we start to become aware of the patterns in our own birthchart, even in the simplest of ways, and begin to watch our development unfolding month by month as described by the planetary patterns spinning out in space (always an amazing thought!), we begin to understand not only our uniqueness, but also how we are part of a greater cosmic whole. One observation that still makes me feel awe and wonder, even after more than 40 years, is that every time I prepare a client's birthchart, I am not only observing the prevailing planetary pattern out in the heavens at the moment of their birth, I am also seeing the patterns in their psyche at the same time, and the detail of the 'information seed' in the acorn that will become the oak tree. So the birthchart is a dramatic demonstration of the inner and outer at the same moment, showing how completely connected we are to the cosmos.

The astrological pattern in the heavens at birth not only describes the gifts, skills and challenges of that individual, but very accurately will outline the lifetime unfolding of that person's development; which of course explains why, when a client comes to see me whether they are 20 or 80, I can tell where they are in their lives, not in terms of level but in terms of pattern. This information is in the form of interlocking matrices of movements of planets in the heavens at that time, interacting geometrically with their birthcharts and giving much symbolic information to the astrologer.

All of this understanding even at a basic level helps us to see a much bigger picture to our lives at any moment. Your individual pattern is inextricably linked with cosmic unfolding; we are all children of the universe, as some wise person once stated. We are even made of stardust, that's how interconnected we are.

The great psychoanalyst Carl Gustav Jung observed the power of this inner-outer birthchart, as he used astrology powerfully with his patients. Astrology formed much of the basis of his theories of synchronicities (inner and outer coincidences) and his theory of psychological archetypes. In a letter to Sigmund Freud on June 12th 1911, he wrote: "My evenings are taken up very largely with astrology. I make horoscopic calculations in order to find a clue to the core of psychological truth. I dare say that we shall one day discover in astrology a good deal of knowledge that has been intuitively projected onto the heavens."

We have 'choice points' all through our days, but always try to operate from a bigger picture. Often undesirable things may happen to us, but it's important not to energise the problem. The more we give a challenging situation our attention, it feeds the negative energetically, and the neuropeptides that are produced from that negative emotion start to cascade through our bodies and invade every cell. Our thoughts produce precise physical changes in our bodies. We can even start to change our neural networks, the road map in our brains, to being less positive when we feel negative emotions, and in addition we are likely to attract more of the same kind of experience and emotion in other ways in our lives, when that's the frequency we are broadcasting. We actually physically extend the neural networks associated with these negative emotions, so instead of Misery Lane we have a Misery Motorway. So we have to become very aware and conscious of our thinking, becoming a 'thought policeman'.

Just to give a personal example, before I knew better, I remember a few years ago a period when most of my machines and devices were failing. My computer had gone into terminal error, my car had to be towed to the scrapyard, the washing machine kept flooding the floor, and I had worked through about five fridges in a year, all of which kept malfunctioning. I was at the end of a period where my home telephone line hadn't worked reliably for two years, with the telephone company unable to find the fault. Living in a place with virtually no mobile signal, all calls to the company had to be made from the far corner of my garden, the only place with a faint signal, often in Biblical rain. The frustration and anger at these daily obstacles had been building, and then finally my heating boiler stopped working during a freezing winter. Phone calls had to be made again from the far corner of a snowy garden to contact a repair company, and when the workman arrived he was extremely intimidating. I don't know whether he had just had a bad day or a bad life, but his attitude was angry and threatening, and I couldn't get him out of the house fast enough; but in a blinding flash I saw how I had actually, from small beginnings, created all of this angst. My frustration and anger had energised the problems, attracting bigger and bigger frustrating and anger-making situations into my life, until finally they reached a crescendo with a very angry, bullying workman in my home. I hadn't been able to sort out my negative emotions, and the outer always must reflect the inner, producing the stream of mechanical/technical breakdowns and culminating in an aggressive workman. Now the inner me needed some serious work.

I sat down for a long meditation that night to release all the anger I felt. Strangely enough, all the technical and mechanical problems started to resolve themselves from that point. It was actually a wonderful lesson to observe how I had created these problems in my own life.

So learn from my example, and when something goes wrong now, I always think 'this is already fixed, things always get fixed.' I will usually take a deep breath, and step back from the situation. If it is something mechanical, like the printer won't work, after taking a breath I set an intention that 'the printer is now working', and it is almost magical how, invariably, the printer then works perfectly.

If it is a human interaction situation, if someone is angry or frustrated or expressing negative emotion in your close company, before reacting, again take a breath, but also a take a moment to ask, 'What would my highest self do in this situation? What is the best I can be here? Can I use love to understand this person better?' Those kinds of questions can help to stop me overreacting too quickly, or acting in a way that is less than optimum. If my negative thinking at any point seems to be gathering momentum, I just imagine a big red STOP traffic sign, and tell myself to stop it, out loud: then I very deliberately turn my thinking to something positive.

If you have a challenge in life that is quite significant and you feel may be ongoing, try to not give it energy and attention, which would tend to spoil your days anyway, but see the problem as very small, peripheral, and faint in your life. Try to not see it as overwhelming and all-consuming, otherwise it will become that. Tell yourself that 'all problems are sorted eventually'. If you can't take any action practically to help, focus on all the wonderful things that are happening in your life so you always see the glass as half-full, Pollyanna-style. Of course, you can use meditation and visualisation to see this problem as dissolving, insubstantial, and becoming so tiny on the horizon that it disappears. If it is a financial challenge, visualise money or gold coins falling from heaven, forming piles of abundance beneath your feet. If it is a health issue, imagine yourself as a being of radiant, shining light, vibrating with energy. See any medical treatment you are having as diamond white light being poured into you, to raise your vibration.

Remember that your outer reality is merely a reflection of your inner reality. The universe is a mirror. So it's pointless blaming people or external circumstances for your situation, as the solution always lies within you. This helps us to take responsibility for our lives.

Another helpful technique with challenges is to 'reframe the problem'. You can ask yourself what is the good in this situation that you're not seeing, or ask what it is teaching you. That can really help to put a positive spin on the problem, to see it as part of your journey of growth.

Importantly, I always start my day with two things, even before I open my eyes. One is my gratitude list, which could be as simple as a comfy pillow, or birdsong in the morning, or rays of sunlight coming into the room, or having certain people in my life. I try to make it different every day. Secondly, I set an intention that I am going to have an awesome day, filled with manifesting magic. This helps me expect miracles through my day, and gives me a feeling of excited anticipation, the perfect manifesting emotion. I say to myself, 'I'm going to experience magic today, that only I will understand.'

As well as feeling gratitude before I open my eyes, through the day I try to take moments every now and then to watch the trees swaying in the wind outside my window, or the birds making nests for their young in spring, and feel filled with gratitude for all that nature has to offer. It helps to reset my emotional state through the day. I will always try to use positive language, describing my life as 'lucky, blessed and abundant'; these are all good messages to reinforce positive chemistry in your body, but also keep a high frequency day to day. You can't just use these practices for one small part of the day, such as a few moments in the morning, but then revert to more negative patterns through the day. You have to continually broadcast that higher frequency of the best that you can be, every day, to attract in the best to your life. In fact, *your frequency and state of being that you are broadcasting all day every day are the most important elements in manifesting*, so you need to become aware of your 'background' or default frequency. We can so often get caught up in the physicality of 'what is now' that surrounds us; but that is merely the result of past thinking and emotions. We can also become obsessed by what we are, or are not, receiving. 'Why haven't I received this yet?' may be a common thought for many of us. Instead of focusing on the present or how much or little you are receiving, try to switch your focus to your broadcasting frequency. You are the creator who now understands their blueprint. You are the master of your state of being and mind.

This language also helps to soften any challenges from the past. We can rewrite our lives, which are only the stories we tell ourselves and others about what happened. You can keep the facts the same, but instead of being the victim of circumstances, you can describe how you triumphed over them. Life doesn't get you down, you will never play the victim, as that is when we are voluntarily giving away our power to whoever treated us badly, in our eyes. The more we tell this story of misery, the deeper the ruts in our neural network become, the more rigidly defined we are by our past, rather than our future. If you keep telling the same miserable small story about your past, energetically you are creating the same miserable small future.

If your past has been challenging, try to loosen the grip of these old emotions, soften them, let them blur somewhat; it is best if you can to even acknowledge responsibility in allowing those things to happen, even if it was unconscious collusion in playing the part of a world-class doormat. The more you can see some responsibility yourself, the more easily you can forgive, let the baggage go, and move on with a lighter step.

Astrology is extremely helpful in seeing that someone's challenging childhood was not just bad luck, but actually provided the fuel to galvanise that person into a life of unique contribution, and giving love back to the world. For instance, I have had several clients who were sexually abused as children, and now work with abused or neglected children as their life's work. They are bringing so much goodness and love to so many children, and I feel sure that their work would not have taken that course without their traumatic childhood experience. They haven't just earned a certificate in childcare, they are operating from a very deep place of being and feeling in their work. So their lives come full circle in a way that gives so much meaning to the original experience; they start to see it as part of their growth, rather than just years of misery. Often this 'full circle' realisation occurs in the astrological consultation when the client can suddenly see the meaning behind their tough childhood, to give them the purpose of their lives; this involves a shift of consciousness occurring there and then, and it is a privilege to simply hold the space for those shifts to take place.

In a moment we are going to start practically building the picture of the future you based on your own individual birthchart, but as well as the visualising you will be doing to bring that into manifestation it's important to take action towards that goal. I remember listening to a Mike Dooley speech at a conference recently, who used the analogy of making your desired result the postcode you punch into your GPS, but he made the point that you actually have to start the car engine and put your car in gear in order to get to that destination. You don't need to know the details of your journey, as the universe (or the GPS) is smarter than we are in sorting that out for us, but we do need to take action in the direction of our goal, and put energy into it.

All of these principles are things that I try to practise in my day-to-day life, so I walk my talk. I've found them all incredibly helpful in moving my life forward in unimaginable ways from my early years, almost like a dream. The more you can think of reality as less hard-edged and more pliable and flexible, as we know from Chapter 3, the easier it becomes to manifest your desires for your future self. We have great opportunities in the coming years to understand this more fully. I feel that some of the ideas I am setting out in this book will simply be common practice in years to come, but as a reader now you have a head start on your destiny.

7 Creating your Future Self

"Do what you love. Know your own bone; gnaw at it, bury it, unearth it, and gnaw it still."

Henry David Thoreau

Part 1

Now you are going to start the important process of defining your future self. This is where you may feel that you are touching something very deep in yourself, so it is important to do this in an uninterrupted place, where you can have some peace to contemplate and be creative.

I would like you to recall a time when you had a dream, something you really wanted to achieve, and made it manifest in your life. All of us will have experienced that, usually many times, but choose something that was significant and exciting for you. You may have been very preoccupied with that dream and certain it was going to happen. You would have imagined yourself in that situation, feeling the success or fulfilment of the experience before it happened. You made the thought a reality.

For me, one of my dreams was emigrating to Canada; I had that dream when I was 16, and eventually achieved it the day after I left university. Over those years from 16 to 21, I read about the beauty of Canada, and I had pictures of the mountains and lakes on the walls of my bedroom. I thought about the space, the big horizons, the fresh air, and the outdoor life. I could imagine myself hiking up mountains and looking out to infinity from the crests. I had no doubt I was going to live there. The *feeling* side of this is the vital ingredient to make this work powerfully for you.

Another example was the dream of buying a small house in France.

I found the area where I wanted it to be: a wild, unspoilt, ancient part of the world. Then I decorated my kitchen in the UK to be in typical French colours of blue and yellow, and had pictures of old French bicycles and fields of lavender on the walls. I imagined myself in the local market chatting to the locals and buying olives, getting my French back to fluency. So I was surrounding myself with that vision, and already stepping into it. I absolutely knew, with the certainty that when you turn on the light switch the light will come on, that this would come to pass. Indeed, within a surprisingly short time, around two months, I saw an advertisement for the perfect place. It ticked all the boxes in terms of my dream.

Take time to savour that memory of when manifesting your dreams has worked in your life, when you made real your dream. Get back into the joy of being successful, happy, excited, or loved and appreciated. You may want to take the time to think of more than one example, whether it is in your work life, personal life, or any strong area of interest that you have. The more examples you can recall of when you have done this in your own life, the more they will give you the confidence that you can manifest whatever you want, as everyone can do this. Focus on the end result of your manifestation, not the details of how you achieved that. That's not your job here, as you will be operating from 3rd dimensional tangible 'efforting', rather than 5th dimensional creating, where this process is almost effortless. In the 5th dimension we lose our sense of time and space. You will undoubtedly already sense this 5th dimension when you are meditating, being in nature, sitting by water, listening to music, or lost in painting or creating something. It is that altered state where we lose a sense of space, time and our own separate identity.

It's important to understand that the emotions we feel are the powerhouse of this, so we are going to be doing this with focus, clarity and a 'heightened emotion', of love, joy, gratitude, or appreciation. You have an excited anticipation that you know what you want is going to manifest. The heightened emotion plus the lost-in-the-moment altered state from our everyday consciousness is what shifts us from 3D to 5D. That is the place we need to create from. It is also why some people find that positive affirmations may not work for them; we need the emotional shift to make a difference. If we are broadcasting these higher emotional states (and it is impossible not to if we are feeling them, as we have seen that we are not completely contained within our bodies), then just like being tuned to 'Radio Abundance' we will attract that as our reality. You can't be tuned to Radio Misery and attract abundance into your life, just as on your own radio you have to be tuned to Classic FM to hear classical music, not the local hard rock station.

Your emotional state is a very crucial part of manifesting. For instance, abundance is an **attitude**, how you feel, rather than how much money you have in your bank account. You can feel abundant simply by being in nature.

Now fill in on an additional sheet of paper to your worksheet some examples of when you have manifested your desires successfully in your life. This will help to remind you of that 'state' that drew the experience towards you.

Now let us talk about the practicalities. Before you write anything, I would like you to light a candle, even burn some incense if you would like to, and then relax into some deep breathing. I would just like to explain a little more about the importance of the breath here. Our thoughts and feelings are in a constant feedback loop, with thoughts being electrical impulses and feelings being magnetic waves. The feeling side is more important; we can be saying positive affirmations, but if our feeling state is slightly agitated or anxious, we cannot achieve 'coherence' in what we are trying to do, and it pulls down our vibration. Actually, the fundamental determinant of our feelings comes from our physiological state. If we are physically relaxed, we are much more likely to have positive emotions than if we have any tensions or stress in the body. The one big thing that can change your physical state within seconds is your breath.

When we are at all anxious, frustrated, or experiencing any negative emotion, our breath tends to be 'incoherent'; that is, it is not smoothly rhythmic, but a series of shallow and irregular breaths. Just try now to close your eyes and focus on your breathing, imagining that you are breathing in and out of your heart. I would recommend that you lightly touch your sternum to help you connect to this heart space, turn inward, and just keep your attention on the slow, deep, rhythmic pace of your breath. Gradually allow a slight pause at the end of each outbreath, so you can drop deeper into your breath and your centre. This is so simple, and it is where you can always find peace. The breath is like a magic wand to calm you, and you always have it with you, wherever you are. Slowing your breathing activates the vagus nerve in the body, which in turn connects to the parasympathetic nervous system, instantly slowing your heart and relaxing your mind and body.

Feel a positive emotion such as love, gratitude or appreciation for all that you have in your life. I often feel emotion for very simple things like fresh air, and clean water, or the breeze on my skin, for I would sadly miss those if I didn't have them; so they are to be appreciated. Sometimes I'm thankful for having arms and legs, lungs and eyes, for they are all miraculous. Notice how your breath deepens even more with this. A yoga teacher many years ago taught me this technique, and now we know that simply doing this for a few minutes reduces our cortisol (stress) levels, and makes all of our body systems work more coherently. It also significantly expands the electromagnetic field around our body. The respected HeartMath Institute in America has a great deal of evidence as to the power of the breath. I would recommend doing this several times a day, so that gradually this becomes your natural default state.

For the purposes of this exercise, I recommend you do this for at least 10 minutes, but for as long as you like to achieve a relaxed, clear state. Don't miss this step, as it is helping you shift from your normal 3D waking state, towards a very relaxed 5D state where you start to blur your sense of time and space.

You are going to be summoning a new possibility into your life from the quantum field, and this will create your future. We used to think that 'manifesting' was an ability limited to magicians and shamans, but we are learning how to do it right here. The big benefit is that you are now working from your own unique template, not just a general modality. You have some very clear guidance.

Firstly I suggest that you get some small pieces of paper. I normally just cut up an A4 piece into about eight smaller pieces, about the size of Post-it notes. The reason for this is that you will just be writing down *one thought or idea* on each piece of paper to maximise the flexibility and creativity of your thinking. You can keep changing the flow of how you are seeing the ideas then.

So far in this book you have used the worksheet to note down the important astrological elements we have discussed. This was an easy way to collect your ideas and thoughts about your Nodal Axis and Midheaven; we are taking the next step in the process now.

I'd like you to write down the words, phrases or sentences that really resonated with you, but do this on separate pieces of paper, using the notes you've made on your worksheet. Particularly identify the meaning of these different areas in your life. If you confidently know other areas of your chart, write these down too. Generate as many of these as you can, keeping each thought separate. The reason for this is that it stops you getting too caught up in left-brained logic. You start by using the more creative right side of your brain in generating the ideas for your pieces of paper, then use the left side of your brain, the more logical side, to build a theme around your future. Separating the two different brain functions makes this very easy.

You should have at least a dozen of these, maybe more, that feel like part of you. Think deeply about the qualities of the signs and houses, and what they say about you. What talents and abilities have you already demonstrated in your life that resonate with the Nodal Axis, or the Midheaven sign? What do you currently do for work, and does that link with your Nodal Axis or Midheaven fully enough? Is there a pattern there? What are your areas of interest in life, or preoccupations, which echo these signs/houses? What are your passions? What lights you up? What makes you happy? What made you happy as a child? When do you feel fulfilled? When do you feel valued and appreciated? What books do you have on your bookshelves? How do you spend your weekends? What qualities and situations does your mind keep going back to? Have you had a spiritual experience that was truly meaningful to you? Do you have any thoughts of a past life where you may have lived out these qualities? Up to this point in life you may well have been largely living out the qualities of your South Node, as that is your default position, what you have already achieved and find easy; or you may have managed to head broadly in the direction of your North Node, but you have almost certainly done this unconsciously and unknowingly. Now, you are becoming a conscious creator, which is much more powerful in manifesting what you want.

Sit with the descriptions or ideas that really mean something to you on a deep level. Now play with the order of these pieces of paper, seeing how changing the order produces different themes or images for you. Separating the ideas can help you to see if one idea keeps drawing your attention more than the others. Do they link together? How much do they reflect what you have already achieved in your life? In this process can you start to see a much bigger vision of who you may become, your future self, but also how this continues a theme that may have been running for several lifetimes (South Node sign and house)? Then you will be starting to see your life from the soul level, not just the day-to-day practical level. This in itself can shift your consciousness.

After playing with the order of your pieces of paper for a while, I suggest putting the ideas linked to the South Node sign and house at the bottom of the table, and the ideas linked to the North Node, sign and house, its planetary ruler and its house, and the Midheaven sign and planetary ruler, all at the top of the table. This helps you to see the direction of soul evolution, or travel, in this lifetime. You're evolving from the South Node qualities of the past to your North Node/Midheaven in this lifetime. For me, the physical separation of these pieces of paper helps me to see this more clearly.

Through this process repeat the simple touching your heart centre and connecting with the breath, finding the peace within, as often as you like, and ask your heart for guidance about what is coming up for you, as it is believed that your heart connects you to your intuition. How many of these ideas can you connect to? In connecting to them, does that take you to another idea that you have distantly thought about, or dreamed of, but up to now never really focused on? Or perhaps you have already taken some steps in that direction, but now with these descriptions it is becoming clearer? Ask your higher self to show you a vision of your future self, and you can even ask for this to be shown to you in your dreams as you fall asleep. Every night I ask to be shown something in my dreams, and it is remarkable what comes through; all free guidance. I recommend that you do this process several times, and keep coming back to it in your mind. Meditate on the combination of the ideas, toss them around in your mind in quiet moments, visualise what could come from these. The alchemy here has to come from you, from your deepest and highest self, to synthesise these thoughts and ideas into your clear life direction. You are actively and consciously co-creating here, with the deepest part of who you are meant to become. The descriptions in this book are merely to stimulate these deeper parts of you, rather than being complete in themselves. They may seem very simple, but you need to meditate on them. This is where the magic actually happens of realising who you really are.

So I'd like you to be creative with this process, generating other ideas that come to you when you dwell on these descriptions. What images, dreams and achievements is this process helping you to see now? Don't rush this process, as this is your life purpose, your reason for being on Earth this time around, that you are contemplating. It may take several days, or even a couple of weeks, to feel you've really nailed it. It's worth the time.

As long as your time of birth is correct, some of these descriptions will resonate deeply. It may well stir something in you that you have never been able to perceive or articulate before. Even having worked with astrology for many years, I remember the awakening I felt when I truly understood the Nodal Axis in my chart. I still recall the goosebumps I felt when it was as if my entire life had fallen into place. If you've never worked with your birth-chart before, it can be like dozens of pieces of a jigsaw that just magically form the whole picture before your eyes. I also had a sense of not just see-ing this life more clearly, but having a feeling of a continuous thread running through lifetimes, building on previous knowledge. Images started to emerge in dreams that built a theme through time and space.

As Patanjali said, "When you are inspired by some great purpose, some extraordinary cause, all your thoughts break their bonds: your mind tran-scends limitations, your consciousness expands in every direction, and you find yourself in a new, great and wonderful world. Dormant forces, faculties and talents come alive, and you discover yourself to be a far greater person than you ever imagined yourself to be."

As part of this process, it's very helpful to just select one quality at a time from either your North Node sign or house to really focus on. Close your eyes and decide the main quality you want to incorporate into your life. Is it financial self-sufficiency (North Node in Taurus)? Is it being more assertive (North Node in Aries)? Feel this deeply in your being. Think about how you can start to live that quality in your life right now, from today. How will it change your day-to-day life? Who will you start to become? Then once you have incorporated that quality into your days, choose another quality and meditate upon how you start to live that one in your life, so you are gradually consciously and deliberately creating the evolutionary North Node growth in your life that you were born to achieve.

This process can galvanise your life. Once you fully understand your life purpose, things will just flow, as you are co-creating with your birthchart. We are now in alignment with our divine plan. Animals and plants have an advantage over us, in that a sheep doesn't have internal debates about whether it should be a sheep, it just gets on with being a sheep. An acorn just gets on with being an oak tree; but our minds either through self-doubt or the desire to conform to the mainstream can get in the way of who we are meant to become.

The Nodal Axis is such a beautiful part of the sacred, secret language of astrology that it makes me feel very moved when I look at this in my clients' charts. I feel enormously privileged that I am perceiving their divine spark and their divine purpose in this life. The birthchart always holds your highest truth. As Deepak Chopra said, quoting the ancient Vedic texts the Upanishads, "You are what your deepest desire is. As is your desire, so is your intention, so is your will. As is your will, so is your deed. As is your deed, so is your destiny."

I'm now going to share with you some examples of how this has worked in the lives of some of my clients.

The first client we will call Jane. In her birthchart we are just going to focus on the elements described above, but as I have mentioned, if you know the meanings of your Sun, Moon, Ascendant and so on, they can also enrich the picture for you. I described the broad symbolism of Jane's Nodal Axis and Midheaven, and their planetary rulers, then asked her to write out each word or phrase that really resonated with her in line with these, on separate pieces of paper. The words and phrases below are what Jane particularly noted from the descriptions:

Her North Node is in Pisces: Creativity, artist, fine perception, quality of light, iridescence, beauty, hypnotic effect, creating altered states in others, inspired, ethereal.

Her North Node is in the 10th house: Career, success, authority, status, reputation, professionalism.

Her North Node Planetary Ruler is Neptune (ruler of the sign Pisces) in the 5th house: (children), inspired creativity, originality, finding oneness in creativity.

Her South Node is in Virgo: Serving day-to-day practical needs, being of service, fretting, anxiety, humility.

Her South Node is in the 4th House: Home, children, nurturing, protecting, caring for family, home base (not out in the world).

Her Midheaven is in Pisces: Ruled by Neptune; creativity, artistry, flowing with life, spiritual inspiration/inspiring others, reminding others through her art of the spiritual side of life/nature.

Jane very much recognised her South Node pull towards the home, keeping a low profile, and caring for others. She adores children (emphasis in the 5th house of children, as her North Node ruler is there). So not only did she spend a lot of her life looking after her own children, but she also worked in low-paid agency jobs looking after other people's children. She also worked as a foster mother for special needs children. Although Jane always loved the children she was working with, the hours were very long, and as the pay was so limited she often struggled to pay bills. She hesitated to pursue her creativity, as she didn't feel she had the confidence in her ability.

I asked Jane to group all the words connected to her South Node – by sign, house and the planetary ruler's house – towards the bottom of the table, and all others connected to her North Node and Midheaven rising up from there, grouped at the top of the table. This helped to give her a sense of direction of 'soul travel', having come in with the skills and abilities of the South Node already, but needing to head towards the North Node and Midheaven. I then asked her to make sentences out of these separate words and phrases, as this really helps to make the direction of travel very clear for her.

These are some of the sentences that she wrote, and I've added in the astrological indicators in brackets to make the process easier for you to see:

It's easy and familiar for me to want to stay at home, not be ambitious, but see to the needs of my family, or other people's children, so they feel nurtured (South Node in the 4th house).

This in turn makes me feel nurtured. I'm often just dealing with the day-to-day practicalities of children, cleaning and cooking (South Node in Virgo). *I always feel pulled back to this, as it's easy for me. However, I recognise it's not enough* (South Node).

I often imagined that I could be a successful artist one day, even though I had never really explored my creativity (North Node and Midheaven in Pisces).

It can feel scary to be out in the world, but I feel it's something I have to do (North Node, virgin territory).

I love beauty, and colour, and beautiful shimmering mermaid-like light, that can feel surreal (Pisces North Node and Midheaven). *That's where I go in my imagination, and that's what I want to explore with colour in art.*

I'd like to use different materials, not just paint, but texture, to express beauty (Pisces North Node and Midheaven, and Neptune in the 5th house of creativity).

I think I may be able to produce something original, if I trust my instincts. It transports me to another place when I think about that, and it would be wonderful to inspire others with that too (Pisces North Node and Midheaven).

I would feel so fulfilled to be a successful professional artist, and have a proper career where I would be respected out in the world (North Node in the 10th house).

This all perfectly reflected in the symbolism of her Nodal Axis and Midheaven.

After Jane's astrology session when I described the importance of the North Node, and we went through the creative exercise above, she started taking some evening classes in painting, and the teacher quickly recognised her talent. She started to develop a very individual style, inspired by her understanding of the North Node by sign and house, and her Midheaven. Her paintings were abstract and ethereal, but with vibrant colour, and often using shimmering reflective materials such as mica or crushed crystals. They were quite magical and hypnotic. You felt pulled into her pictures; they were almost like mandalas. She started to hold local exhibitions of her work that did very well, and eventually she set up her own small art gallery for her work. Jane received many accolades for her art. Her work was even selected for exhibition at some national galleries. She was now out in the world (North Node in the 10th house), expressing her creativity (North Node and Midheaven in Pisces) in her own individual way, and building her reputation. She also does some voluntary work as an art therapist, helping special-needs children to express themselves. This was also incorporating her North Node ruler Neptune in the 5th house of children and creativity, as well as her South Node in the 4th house in a very positive way of 'motherhood' and nurturing, but being out in the world at the same time.

Jane was strongly supported by her loving family (South Node in the 4th house), and now felt that she was really moving forward and making something of her life. She now had a sense of purpose and meaning, which motivated her every day, rather than feeling she was 'staying small' in her South Node role.

There were many other parts of the chart that supported this direction, but if we just take the Nodal Axis and Midheaven alone, we can understand so much of the direction of travel that her soul has to take in this lifetime. It pares it down to the bare bones, before we add on the other layers of astrological information in the whole birthchart.

I'd suggest that as the next step in your process, write a narrative just as Jane did to take your ideas/visions to the next level where it can start to feel more achievable. Writing things down takes thinking to a more definite level; for instance in studies done with New Year's resolutions, there is a much higher level of success amongst those people who write them down versus those who don't, as it is one step closer to manifesting them.

I went through the same creative process with another client, let's call her Maria, where we particularly focused on her Nodal Axis.

Maria came from a home where her father was extremely angry and dominating, and who favoured her sister over her. So there was a constant feeling of 'not good enough', and needing to stay quiet, while actually acting as the peacemaker in the family. This was reflected in her South Node in Libra (the go-between, the people pleaser), in her 11th house of lovability. This strongly suggested that Maria was suppressing any of her own needs to not only keep the peace and deny any assertive feelings of her own (Libra tendency is to be 'other-directed'), but because of the 11th house position of her South Node (need to stay as a people pleaser). This created a need for constant appreciation, love and reassurance from others as to her own self-worth, as she never received enough support for this from her parents. Her South Node planetary ruler is Venus (this rules Libra), and this is in her 2nd house of self-worth. So this reinforced the picture of low self-worth, a low sense of lovability, and the constant need for support from others (11th house = friends).

However, her North Node is in Aries, in the 5th house. Aries is the sign of the warrior, the pioneer, the courageous person who can go solo, be an entrepreneur. The 5th house is the house of creativity, and/or children. Her North Node ruler, Mars, is in Virgo, in her 10th house of career. Her Midheaven is in Virgo, a practical, detailed Earth sign, often connected to artisan skills and working with tangible materials, reflecting the Earth sign. She started to develop beautiful, original designs for ceramics and wall tiles. They were very detailed, and in beautiful colours (reflecting her South Node in Libra, beauty, ruled by Venus = colour). She was very perfectionist about her work (Virgo), but was determined to create very different designs, and be a pioneer in this, reflecting her North Node in Aries (pioneer, go it alone) in the 5th house of creativity. She began to feel fulfilled, and recognised that she was now living her passion and expressing her creativity in a way she had never contemplated before. The unconfident, shy, unsure Maria had been replaced by an artist who was truly blossoming, a joy to see.

Let's take a final example of someone we will call John. He has his South

Node in Virgo in the 2nd house, which suggests someone who has a pull from the past towards financial security, and that money is important to him. He may worry (Virgo) and fret about this a great deal, and likes to analyse (Virgo) his financial situation. No surprise then that he was drawn towards accountancy; he excelled at detail (Virgo), he was interested in finance, and Virgo likes to be of practical service to others. His interest in finance was reinforced by his Midheaven in Taurus (banking), and he had become a very successful investment banker. His Midheaven ruler is also in Taurus. Taurus is 'fixed Earth', so commonly associated with banking and wealth, and also luxury. He loved beautiful things and expensive cars, and on meeting him I sensed that he exuded wealth. However, he felt that there was something missing. His North Node is in Pisces in the 8th house, a very different part of him. Pisces is the most spiritual, ethereal sign, and the 8th house is connected to alternative healing. This is where he would find his purpose, a long way away from the world of banking.

Interestingly, the 8th house is also connected to giving financial advice to others; although that had been part of his role, it wasn't expressing the Pisces side of his nature; so he was now understanding that he had to live the 8th house symbolism at a much deeper, more spiritual level in order to feel fulfilled.

He began to take some Reiki courses, and found that he had a natural ability to read energy (North Node Pisces). He felt this was a much deeper part of him than he had ever explored before; and he developed a fascination for energy and working with the physical body (Taurus Midheaven). The ruler of his North Node, Neptune, is in his 3rd house, so it was important for him not only to practise spiritual healing but also to write about it (3rd house = communication) and start to develop a blog and a loyal following. He eventually left the wealthy world of banking, gave up his expensive life-style, and started to live much more simply in following his North Node of spiritual abundance, rather than just falling back on his South Node of material abundance. He had found his purpose, and a deeper, more meaningful way to live. The banking world became like a hollow shell for him, he said. He ultimately became a spiritual counsellor too, reflecting his North Node in the 8th (the spiritual consultant) and the ruler of his North Node being in the 3rd house of communication.

We can see in these examples that you don't need to understand all the complexities of astrology to find your direction of soul growth in this lifetime. Everything you need is in this book, and it can spark something in you that is priceless.

So go back to your pieces of paper, imagining our direction of soul travel from the South Node to the North, and taking the Midheaven into account. Then write out some sentences that come naturally to you, incorporating the symbolism as described in this book. You may also want to add to the ideas that occur to you, which you feel are in line with your direction of soul growth. This should start to give you a much clearer idea of your life purpose, which is what your Nodal Axis is all about. This process should start to throw your life into 'high relief', seeing an underlying pattern that you couldn't have previously articulated, but has been a powerful undertow in your life.

This is helping you to get very clear on that 'future self' that you want to step into, to fulfil your life purpose. The second part of this is to then set an intention, while generating the heightened emotion that is part of that picture. What we are doing here is using your unique astrological potential for your soul's evolution, and then using what we know about how reality is formed via intention as described in Chapter 3, to bring your highest potential into manifestation.

Part 2

Keeping your 'soul purpose' in mind from now on, start to think about what elements of that vision you would like to start to manifest. Keep your desires consistent with your soul purpose, always, in order to be 'on strategy' for this life. At this stage of the process we are moving from *qualities, essences, and direction of soul growth, to the actual definition of the manifestation of those things in this life for you*. What form would you like them to take? If you have the North Node in Cancer or the 4th house, your focus may be on creating a loving family home. Or if you are meant to be a teacher, with the North Node and/or Midheaven in Sagittarius, what kind of teacher? In a primary school? In an Indian village? In a university, or in a less formal setting? Try to get into the feelings of already being that person, and living it. You are already there.

So I would recommend that you get as clear as you can on what you want to start to manifest, and write it down somewhere so that you will be constantly aware of it. Is it being a leader with an international organisation helping third world countries? Is it being an innovator in new technology that will help people's health, via vibrational medicine? Is it simply being there for your family and creating a loving secure home, and not being out in the world? Is it becoming a writer, or successful social media blogger to disseminate important information?

Writing it down not only helps you clarify exactly what you want, but also sharpen the setting of your intention.

Then go deeper into your vision. If you have the North Node in the 3rd house or Gemini, this is about communication, and so how do you want that to manifest? Speaking to global audiences? Writing a best-selling book? Having a strong social media following? Clearly define what success means to you. Write down what, where and when, in as much detail as you like. Never concern yourself with how you are going to get there, as the universe is much smarter than you are in delivering that. Opportunities can come in 'leaps' which you couldn't have imagined. Your focus here is to define your vision, and keep holding and broadcasting that vision both to yourself and out to the world. That will now become your guiding light.

It is helpful to not only write this down in words, but see it in images. You can frequently visualise this in your mind, and you can also collect images to put around your home to constantly remind you and inspire you. Every time you see these, it is the feeling of joy/success/exhilaration/happiness/ love that is most important to amp up your manifestation. It requires both the rational setting of your goal, then emotionally stepping into imagining you are already living it. That heightened state of being is already within you. Both parts are key.

So if you want to write a best-selling book, imagine perhaps that you are standing in front of an audience of hundreds of people, talking about it, and the cover has gold stars on the front to signify your success. Our subconscious responds to images like this, even simple ones, as it works on symbolism such as we experience in our dreams. Remember to feel on top of the world as you do this, soaring with success and achievement.

Once you can start to create these heightened emotions, it is very important to live from that place every day. Yes it's important to recall the details of your vision several times a day, for instance, standing in front of a large audience. However, we have other things we have to think about in a day, so as ongoing background emotion, try and retain that *feeling* of ecstatic success and achievement. That then becomes the frequency of what you are broadcasting out to the world, and you are more likely to pull the manifestation towards you quickly. Think of yourself as a confident, successful speaker. If you can, take small steps towards that. Start offering to do local talks to small audiences, and gradually this will build. Have an overwhelming focus on your intention that you will not be distracted from. Cultivate a sense of absolutely knowing that you are pulling this destiny towards you, without doubt.

I will always start and end my days by revisiting the vision of what I am on the way to achieving. I deliberately do that while still sleepy, especially before I open my eyes or even move in bed in the morning, as you are in a very open and slightly altered state then. The mind doesn't differentiate between visualising and remembering, so it helps to manifest if you see this as **remembering** what you have just achieved; it is much more powerful to feel this as if it has happened a **few days ago**, rather than something in the future; that gap in time keeps pushing the manifestation away from you. This is very important.

Sometimes for fun as part of the picture, I will imagine myself being congratulated warmly, hugged, and slapped on the back; it is just extraordinary how people through the day do just that, even if they do it virtually via social media. I don't even define why they are congratulating me; it comes for a variety of reasons. Try it – again, it's all for free, and you are building both your manifesting muscles and your confidence.

You can never create successfully from a feeling of 'lack'. So if you are dreaming about success and abundance from a wistful feeling of 'well, that would be nice, but I can't imagine it happening to me, as I'm not smart/ young/old/attractive enough...' then you are not stepping into the heightened emotion that is a vital part of the process. Also, you are experiencing separation between you and your desired outcome. You are energetically pushing away the very thing you are wishing for. Your everyday energy, frequency and vibration are the vital ingredients here. Keep tuned to 'Radio Abundance'.

A phrase I try to repeat to myself often during every day is: 'my life is so great now, how could it be even better?' The appreciation of this phrase means that the universe keeps on giving to you. It is a state of excited anticipation that helps to express gratitude for all you have. Even if life is currently very challenging, there will always be something you can be grateful for now, even if it is just clean water and sunshine, and you can build your gratitude from there. An 'attitude of gratitude' seems to be one of the most powerful tools we can use to bring any of our desired dreams to manifestation. It sets our frequency at the right level. As some wise person once said, "If you're not already grateful for what you have, why do you want any more?"

Also start to live the part, step into that life as fully as you can – NOW. Can you already live internally as that future self that you wish to become? Can you start to live the qualities you have identified from the Nodal Axis/Midheaven exercise? Can you start to surround yourself in your home with images of that future life, just as I did with summoning a new French home? It then becomes much more real and easier to imagine that you are already there.

Remember, no wavering, even to yourself, or you have just withdrawn your intention and have to start again, and this is a cumulative process. You are actually building new neural networks in your brain to reflect that desired self, as the heightened emotion produces different biochemistry in our bodies, and in turn that can change the physical structure of our neural network. Then, in that feedback loop, we are more likely to pull the manifestation towards us, as our brains are already primed for that experience, and our emotions are tuned to 'Radio Success'. Successful people live this way all the time.

There always has to be coherence between your thoughts and the emotions, so you can't tell yourself you are a loser and it never works for you, while generating the emotions of achievement and joy. One is directly linked to the other, and that is why you have to keep both pointed in the same direction of your dream. We can use these simple techniques to help manifest anything we want in our lives, but the subject of this book is principally how to bring to blossom your 'dharma', your purpose for being on this Earth this time around.

So revisit the ideas and thoughts that have come out of the creative exercise above. You can of course include other ingredients of your birthchart if you feel confident of their meaning, particularly your Ascendant sign if you know that, always keeping in mind the context of your soul's evolution, your Nodal Axis, which you now know. From that rich mix, I would suggest that you develop a very clear 'intention' statement that will become the foundation for you. I would like you to think deeply about the 'future you', whom you are going to become very soon. However, write your intention in the *present* tense, as your vision, energetically, has already been achieved. If you write in the future tense, you will keep pushing it away from you in time. This is a very important point. If we see it in the future, there is a gap in time, and it has the feeling of always being elusive, or we feel that we may never quite reach it. This can reinforce the feeling of lack. As I mentioned above, place the manifestation just a **few days ago, in the immediate past**, so you are still feeling exhilarated by it. This is super-important for your manifesting success. In this way it seems much easier to access the emotion, as you already have achieved that feeling of soaring success, or sheer joy, or complete fulfilment. It is right here right now, and you've already done it. You are now celebrating how great this feels.

So your intention statements are always stated in the present, and may be:

- **"I am a brilliantly successful international coach and speaker"**
- **"I'm giving underprivileged children all the love and care they need"**
- **"I'm loving the success of my best-selling book"**

See whatever your intention is as already happening, having just begun a few days ago. Just step into that life, right now. It's as if you've created an energetic hologram that you can just step into. Spookily enough, that is exactly what you are doing. This will become the guiding light for your actions that will all fall in line with that intended reality.

Intention has been well researched and documented over the last few years by many authors, so we have much evidence of its power. Lynne McTaggart is the dominant figure in this, and I would highly recommend her book, *The Intention Experiment*, to dispel any doubts you may have as to the power of this. Dr Wayne Dyer had a wonderful statement about this too, as he said: "I'll see it when I believe it," rather than, "I'll believe it when I see it." That's why you have to live from the future event backwards, imagining that it is already achieved.

Historically we have considered thoughts to be wafty, ethereal things that don't really matter; but thoughts carry information that constantly interact with the quantum field and shape our reality. So what is the difference between ordinary thinking and intention? Our ordinary thinking typically is not well disciplined. We have a series of random thoughts through the day, and have to react to many, many inputs. It has been calculated that we have around 90,000 thoughts every single day, and they will be hopping around between work subjects, shopping lists, e-mails and phone calls you have to make, and planning your weekend social activities. Generally in the average person they are pretty scattered, as our modern life is complex and fast-moving.

Intention is different. It isn't just being consciously aware of your thinking; it is deliberately directing your thinking towards a desired outcome. The difference is focus, desire and willpower. It is like a laser beam, where you are very conscious and very clear about the end result, with a sense of momentum about it. Thinking back to our description of the 'observer effect' in Chapter 3, it seems clear that intentions are the most powerful way of influencing that point when consciousness turns into matter, or an event in your life. The observer effect clearly demonstrates that the observer is co-creating reality; that focus is highly efficient at manifesting your desired future.

I want to revisit the idea of *convergence* here; you are focusing your *mind*, your *will* and your *emotional state*, coherently, on your desired outcome, all within the context of your Nodal Axis and Midheaven. As all matter condenses from the quantum field, matter appears at the point where the quantum field is most intense: that is, where it has been activated by your focus and intent. It is the observer effect at its most powerful. In Chapter 3 when describing the latest scientific understanding in how reality works, we now understand, thanks to the wonderful work of the HeartMath Institute, that our own individual magnetic field is constantly interacting with the Earth's geomagnetic field in a constant feedback system. Each of us is feeding the Earth's field with our own magnetic field, the quality of which is determined by our physical state and emotions, and we are constantly receiving information back from the field. This could be why intention is so powerful, because we are not only saying it to ourselves, we are broadcasting it into the Earth's field. It could also be why if you have others supporting you in your intention, the cumulative effect is more powerful, because of this more focused interaction with the field. Thoughts and intentions are starting to look less ethereal, and have more of a scientific, energetic basis with this understanding. We may be starting to discover another fundamental law of the universe, like gravity.

There is a famous experiment conducted by Cleve Backster, a colleague of Deepak Chopra, in the 1970s. He wanted to test how a plant would react to a threatening act. So he connected electrodes to a leaf of the plant, and wondered what he could do that may provoke a reaction in the plant. He decided he would burn the leaf, and searched around the laboratory for some matches. He did indeed burn the leaf, but the big jump in the electrical readings had already begun *when he had the thought of burning the leaf,* which in some way the plant had perceived. This shows that the real power in his interaction with the plant was when it registered his *intention,* rather than the physical act of burning. We may think that the physical act would produce the stronger reaction, but it was the intention, that focus of apparently 'wafty' thoughts, that made the plant react.

Dr William Tiller, a physicist at Stanford University, has conducted many experiments in which he asked experienced meditators to focus intention on altering the pH of water from distances of several miles. Sometimes they were asked to increase the pH, other times to decrease it; but however many times they did this, the water pH changed in line with their intention. He even experimented by asking the meditators to send intention to accelerate the development of a firefly's larvae from 2,000 miles away, again with clear success. This demonstrates how powerful our thoughts are in affecting matter.

Another example of this is with a friend of mine; let's call her Ann. She had been suffering from a serious auto-immune disease for many years, and had seen many specialists and therapists, none of whom had really been able to help her. Then one day she contacted a homeopath who lived thousands of miles away, and the homeopath recommended that she take a very deep remedy which she thought may help. She put it in the post that night, but it took five days to reach Ann. However, straight after the phone call, Ann's healing had already begun in quite a dramatic way. She knew this would be her solution, and by the time the remedy arrived, her auto-immune condition of decades was already receding. That shows the incredible power of intention on behalf of the homeopath, that she absolutely focused on Ann's healing, and transmitted that energetically, five days ahead of the actual remedy being taken.

Both of these are strong examples of the power of intention, and Lynne McTaggart's work contains many, many more that are statistically significant.

So the vital step in this process is getting very clear on what you want, and setting a clear statement of intention. Remember you have a major advantage here, as you are using your unique birthchart in this process, and intention is most powerful when *aligned to your own life's destiny,* and the divine organising intelligence of the universe. You then have the cosmos at your back. This is co-creation at its absolute best, and now you can become a master of that. You have all the ingredients from this book to be the best you can be, at any moment.

So what is happening here is that we are taking your life's blueprint, your birthchart, as your desires will naturally fall from that at any point in your life. Indeed, the birthchart does not describe the end of the story (as your life is your own to live out in terms of how you play your music), but describes the urges, desires, needs and ambitions in various areas of your life at any one time. In this book we are focusing on the deepest part of your chart, your Nodal Axis and soul's life purpose. The more your life can move towards that, the better your life will work. This will give you a feeling of clear vision and meaning in your life. **So in this process we are combining this life theme from your unique blueprint with what we now understand scientifically and practically about creating our own reality**. In addition to your life purpose, we are adding in the ingredients of a clear intention, focus, willpower and a heightened emotional state; these are all the elements we need to bring our desires into reality, quickly.

It has been using the combination of my astrological knowledge together with the understanding of how we create our reality in quantum, scientific terms, then using a simple creative technique that has really made this process so powerful. So this feeling of 'stepping into the desired you' with complete trust and confidence is very important. We have freewill in terms of the level at which we play our music; you now have all the tools you need to make your future inspired.

Now let's work backwards from that future to help cement it. Start to think about what you would like your legacy to be, and imagine it's your 85th birthday party, and a wonderful celebration of your life. Visualise all the people who are there, the speeches that are made about you, the things that are said, the love you receive, and all you have achieved in your life to make the world a better place. Use the ideas and thoughts from your worksheet and pieces of paper. Take that inspiration and develop those ideas further. What can you see for yourself, as your future self? People will be hugging you, congratulating you, celebrating your legacy, the amazing things you have used your life to achieve. What are they? Take time to remember all the great things you have achieved, the ways you have helped people in the world. How have you made a difference? How have you made the world a better place with your unique contribution, in line with your North Node and Midheaven? How far have you been able to go? Remember that if your North Node is in the 4th house your life focus may not be out in the world, but with your family. Equally if it is in the 12th house, your purpose may be lived out behind the scenes. Your life can be just as fulfilled, as long as you are following the line of your Nodal Axis.

Now immediately write down all the feelings and thoughts from the elevated vision you have just experienced. Note down all the wonderful things others were saying about you, and the compliments you received on your achievements. These gifts and talents are an innate part of you. The most important aspects are the emotions you are feeling, as they are what you have to keep revisiting. This has been a life of joy, fulfilment, purpose and happiness. You have all you need now to make that a reality.

It's important as part of this process to rewrite your early life too, as we need to be satisfied with our whole life. If your childhood has been challenging, it is easy to feel like a victim. We were young and powerless, and awful things may have happened around us or even to us, which felt overwhelming. We may have developed survival techniques which are now tripping us up, like being very emotionally well-defended, which gets in the way of all close relationships. However, the story we tell ourselves about our lives is vital in not only the way we see ourselves, but in how others see us. If we feel like a victim and a loser, those themes tend to continue through our lives; we attract yet more experiences where we come off as the loser.

However, although we can't change the events in our lives, we can change the way we react to them. Thinking about those challenging circumstances, instead of feeling like a victim, we can feel like a hero, a survivor of our lives. Against all the odds, we came out of those situations and triumphed; we got a good job, a home, maybe even got married. We won; we didn't crumble. The challenge didn't beat us. So turn around how you see the events, and how you handled them, so you see yourself as a hero of your own life. Look back down the mountain and congratulate yourself. If you can truly change your feelings to reflect this, you will start to notice that everyone around you treats you like a winner too. You are someone who uses challenges to grow, not to feel overwhelmed. Everything shifts.

Astrologically, no one is born with a blank sheet of paper – no one is born neutral. Everyone enters this life with challenges already marked in their birthcharts. These are necessary ingredients for our growth, and some astrologers believe that they reflect our 'soul contracts' that we have signed up to, which are clearly reflected in our birthcharts. So difficult childhoods are never just by chance. They set us up for a series of experiences and journeys which may be part of your North Node and Midheaven symbolism, to come full circle and bring light back into the world, using your childhood experience as the fuel. It will be this that drives you to fulfil your North Node destiny. I truly get shivers when I see this in my clients' charts. If they have experienced physical abuse as a child, they will often have the urge to help disadvantaged children in some way. They will help many dozens, hundreds or even thousands of children, and bring their unique compassion and empathy to the work. They have changed the world for the better, as their childhood experience set them up to do this work. They have come full circle, and fulfilled their destiny. I feel I am holding sacred space in having these conversations with my clients, seeing a much bigger picture than being stuck in childhood pain. Indeed, the Nodal Axis can even give us a vision beyond this lifetime.

If we don't do this, then life wins. We allow circumstances to defeat us, and define us as angry, bitter, insecure, unhappy and unfulfilled. This is a very wasted experience, but what is most important here is that the only person who really suffers here is YOU. You are with yourself 24/7, experiencing the turmoil of these negative emotions, which of course then draws more negative experiences towards you.

We are living in wonderful times now that we can have the tools to empower ourselves, and it is not difficult. It just requires taking the time, and making our focus a conscious practice. By starting simply with our intention exercises, we can start to flex our manifesting muscles. Then we can be truly audacious in our goals. Why not aim high? If we aim high, then even if we only achieve 80% of what we are setting our sights on, then we are still a lot further on in our lives. I believe that with the astrological patterns we have over the next few years, we will start to understand the power of thought, emotion and intention much more fully as we start to live in a world where we appreciate how pliable our energy is. You will have a head start on that as a reader who understands one of the deepest parts of their birthchart.

I have always recognised that your birthchart gives you your pattern, but your consciousness determines your level of manifestation. Increasingly, I am seeing this as suggesting parallel timelines; there are infinite possibilities through any lifetime, but at any one point in time there are only several probable outcomes operating at different levels, but all reflecting the prevailing astrological patterns in your birthchart at that time. For instance, if Saturn in its 29-year orbit is coming to conjunct the Midheaven of a chart, there are several levels of manifestation for this, but *all* will be around the area of career or social status. This transit is not about romantic life, health or children, the focus is the person's expression in the world, principally via their work. So the astrology of the moment narrows down the options from 'infinite' to particular areas of life experience, and the meaning behind the experience. In this case, it is about the expression of your essential self via your work. However, our level of consciousness determines the level at which this symbolism is expressed.

Therefore, if you are not expressing your essential self fully enough, this is the wake-up call for you to do so. It can feel quite karmic, as this is very much the aspect of 'you get what you deserve'. So if you have been cheating the system, or have been involved in dishonest activity, this is the time when you can experience your fall. I mentioned in my first book that the very month that this became exact in US President Nixon's birthchart, the Watergate scandal in which he had been involved was discovered, and he was threatened with impeachment. So these are very negative expressions. However, if you have been working conscientiously and diligently, and in the right area in terms of expressing your Nodal Axis and Midheaven, this can be the culmination of your career. You can feel like you have climbed a mountain, and still have many responsibilities, but have a sense of satisfaction and purpose that you have achieved a great deal, and helped the world too. It's all down to the choices we make. So the possibilities at that time are all around what you've earned in your career, and that becomes very clear.

I think that many of us already have a sense of parallel timelines on a day-to-day basis. Those times when you may have lost your car keys, and you look everywhere for them, then find they turn up in the most improbable place, like the vegetable rack (where I found mine one day!). Or conversely you've looked repeatedly in all the obvious places, then you turn around and find them lying on the worktop right in front of you, where you know you have looked many times. This 'slippage' I feel in a simple way is how we experience parallel timelines. Now, if I lose my car keys, I simply set an intention that: 'I intend that my car keys are now easy for me to find' – and it works like a dream. Just try it, it's all for free. I use intentions a lot during my day, especially the 'this is easy' one. Always state your intentions out loud, especially your important future vision ones, as it is vibrationally stronger than thinking them.

However, the parallel timelines I'm describing may even go beyond this scale. The more we understand our birthcharts and start to live 'strategically', the better our lives will work; but the parallel timelines principle can create a quantum leap in our lives that is such a jump that it's hard for us to imagine. It will always reflect your birthchart, but as we are entering a major time of evolutionary leaps, the universe may deliver something so much higher than our limited minds could envisage. This is where your future self enters completely new ground. We may even start to develop new abilities, such as channelling and telepathy, as being the norms; energetically we become lighter. In understanding the principles set out here as the 'new normal', we will be able to shift between parallel lifetimes much more easily, like changing gears in our car. In fact when you shift your frequency and raise your consciousness, other realities start to become perceptible and accessible to you that you had never imagined.

So instead of feeling so solid, start to think of yourself as an alchemist, and a shape-shifter, in a holographic reality. These are the times, astrologically, that we are entering now.

8 Lunations, Triggers in the Bigger Plan

"The atoms of our bodies are traceable to stars that manufactured them in their cores and exploded these enriched ingredients across our galaxy, billions of years ago. For this reason, we are biologically connected to every other living thing in the world. We are atomically connected to all atoms in the universe. We are not figuratively, but literally, stardust."

Neil deGrasse Tyson, Astrophysicist and Cosmologist

You have come a very long way since you started to read this book. You now understand a great deal more about who you are, and why you are here. In astrology, there is much to learn about the rest of your birthchart, in terms of how it unfolds through your life, and how it is triggered by 'transits'. These are the planets moving around in their orbits, and forming aspects to your natal planets.

We're not going to get into detail about those here, as you can follow them through all of my video, newsletter and regular social media blog updates. These are all very important for your constant unfoldment, but we are all experiencing different aspects at different times, depending on the pattern in our birthchart. These form complex matrices, and the understanding of their meaning takes some years to fully master, but here we are going to concentrate on a regular monthly aspect of astrology that is easy for you to follow in your own chart, but very important in your development.

You already understand that we have focused principally on your own Nodal Axis that was formed at the time of your birth by the Moon's path cutting the ecliptic. However in this chapter rather than talking about the Moon at the time of your birth, we're now going to look at the **current movement of the Moon through the heavens in its orbit**, and how these regular timing triggers are all part of the blossoming of the future you. You can start to follow these monthly unfoldments from today, simply by knowing where these movements of the Moon are happening in your own birthchart. You can track these movements by following my YouTube videos (pamgregoryastrology), or by subscribing to my monthly newsletter at www.pamgregory.com as I give a list of current movements of planets for the month at the end of each of these newsletters, or simply by an Internet search for any day. Then you start to feel on a month-by-month basis how your development is interacting with the cosmos, and begin seeing your soul's evolution start to unfold. It's very exciting, and very easy for you to follow.

Here we're going to focus on New Moons, Full Moons and Eclipses, which are all called 'lunations', because they all are linked to the Moon, or *luna* in Latin. We all experience these, although they fall in different parts of our unique birthcharts each time, and aspect or trigger our astrological patterns in individual ways. Although there is a whole hierarchy of complex interlocking planetary cycles, these lunations which happen regularly every month bring things into your life so you move forward on your path of destiny. See these as stepping stones in your development, each adding to the rich picture of you. If you start to observe these month by month it becomes fascinating to see your life unfold. If you are aware of these rhythmic monthly movements of the Moon, you feel less separate, more connected to divine intelligence, as you watch events in your life ebb and flow, but all following divine timing. Even that in itself can raise your consciousness.

At a fundamental level, it is believed that the Moon actually created life on Earth. The Moon's orbit helps to stabilise the Earth's orbital 'wobble', to give a relatively stable climate for life to flourish. We know life began as simple micro-organisms in the ocean, and then learned to adapt to dry land by living on the shore line, where they alternatively became dry and wet with the tides, to gradually enable them to move onto dry land completely, after tens of thousands of years of adaptation. It is believed by many scientists that the crashing of the waves due to the tides actually produced precursor nucleic acids, which ultimately became building blocks for DNA and life on Earth. So the Moon is vital to life.

As we saw earlier in Chapter 3, the orbits of the Moon and Earth are intricately linked to the biological and physiological processes of all life, from micro-organisms to humans; they determine melatonin and cortisol levels, blood pressure, red blood cell production, heart rate, uric acid levels, temperature, and many other biomarkers that have a rhythm connected to the movements of the Moon and Earth around the Sun. Remarkably, these daily orbital rotations are even encoded at an atomic level in our protein structures. We are inextricably linked to these cycles, and life on Earth is completely dependent upon them. There are other more obvious physical effects too; for example it is well documented that many people find it harder to sleep on the nights building up to the Full Moon.

The Moon in astrology represents your feelings and emotions, and describes what you need to feel instinctively comfortable, day to day. In your birthchart, if you have the Moon in a water sign (Cancer, Scorpio and Pisces) you may be particularly sensitive and emotional, whereas in an Earth sign (Taurus, Virgo and Capricorn) your emotions may be steadier. In air signs (Gemini, Libra and Aquarius) you usually need to connect socially to people in order to feel emotionally satisfied, and in fire signs (Aries, Leo and Sagittarius) you need to experience inspiration, action or creativity to feel satisfied in life. For instance, if you have a natal Moon in Pisces you may need to meditate and candle-gaze to feel instinctively comfortable; if it is in Aries you may need to climb a mountain, and be physically active.

However, even by transit (the daily motion of the Moon), the Moon affects our daily ebb and flow. Feelings and emotions are much more likely to run high as we approach a Full Moon (the peak of the cycle). As well as many people finding it harder to sleep there tends to be a higher crime rate and mental disturbance at a Full Moon. So the rhythm of the Moon in the heavens has a very direct physical effect on our state of being.

Eclipses are even more powerful than this, and that is why the ancient peoples had ceremonies at these times. As the Eclipses create a pull on the electromagnetic field of the Earth and therefore change it, sensitive people are able to more easily download information from a higher source. The Eclipses act as portals as the veil thins. Eclipses were highly respected in ancient times, and if you start to follow these repeating cycles, you will observe how powerful they can be in your life. Eclipses have a powerful link to the Nodal Axis, as Eclipses can only happen within 18 degrees of the *transiting* Nodal Axis. They can act as pivot points to jump you forward on your path of destiny, particularly if they aspect any planets in your chart. So they are directly linked to the current transiting Nodal Axis at any time, which represents our collective destiny. However, in seeing where these Eclipses fall in your individual birthchart, you can then determine their meaning for you. This is what we are going to look at in this chapter.

Astronomically, a Solar Eclipse happens when the Moon passes between the Sun and the Earth, partially or totally blocking the light from the Sun. This can only happen at a New Moon. A Lunar Eclipse is when the Earth passes between the Sun and the Moon, thus throwing a shadow on the Moon. This can only happen at a Full Moon.

It is very easy to follow these lunations; you don't need to work out any complex geometry, or know any more astrology than we have discussed so far in this book. Be aware that as we move through the year, the New Moons move progressively through the signs from Aries in springtime, all the way to Pisces in February/March. We experience each of these lunations differently, depending on our unique birthchart.

Think of your own birthchart as a beautiful mandala, which is like a spider's web. Whenever any aspect falls in your chart it causes the entire web to wobble. It affects the whole. So don't see these lunations as discrete, separate happenings in your life, but rather contributing to your organic life development. See these monthly developments as working towards your North Node and Midheaven expression in the world. Every planetary transit in your chart is helping you move towards your soul purpose.

Now we are going to have to understand just a little more about the framework of the chart in order to observe these New Moons, Full Moons and Eclipses. As we have to understand where each lunation falls in our birthchart in order to determine the meaning for us, it's very helpful to know which signs come after which, so just refer to the table in Chapter 4. Remember, this keeps you moving around the chart in an anti-clockwise direction, and also when you are looking for a particular degree, it's very helpful to know if you are at the beginning of the sign or the end. There are 30° in each sign, so for instance, if you are looking for 9° Virgo, you will know that this is closer to the beginning of Virgo than the end. If you are looking for 27° Virgo, that will be very close to the end of the sign, in fact only 3° from the end.

It's always very important to do this in TWO steps; don't just rush to see which house, for instance, the New Moon is in. Firstly, always work around the outside ring to find the correct astrological **sign**, taking care not to muddle up signs like Virgo and Scorpio where the symbols can look similar. Then find the exact degree you are looking for, let's say it's 2° Taurus. You will know that this is very close to the beginning of Taurus, and you will also know by now that Taurus follows Aries, so you won't make an error. Now, as the second step, see which **house** that falls in in your birthchart; then you can refer to the meanings from the table on page 45, to know what you can anticipate coming up in your life. It's important to say that if the aspect of the New Moon you are looking for is very close to the end of a house, *if it is within three degrees of the next house cusp*, I consider that to be 'rushing into' the next house, and will read it as the next house meaning, rather than the one in which it falls technically.

Now you can start to identify what any New Moon or Full Moon means for you. These will be expressed as the degrees of a sign, for instance, 3° Aries.

A New Moon represents a new beginning. Remember this is just a seed you are sowing in that area of life; it will take a little while to come to blossom, but just watch how that idea, conversation, phone call, or article you read, can prompt something that is the new beginning which then becomes an important part of your destiny and development over time. As well as the general meaning I will be giving to any New Moon in my videos and newsletters, you will have your own specific new beginning in a particular area of life for you. Will it be a new beginning in a romantic relationship if it falls in your 5th house? Or in your career, 10th house? Or in your health, 6th house? As you watch how these patterns unfold month by month, you can start to see *how the cosmos affects your life very directly.* That is very exciting. Each New Moon is a perfect time to set a new intention of what you want to manifest within the context of the energy of that New Moon, as well as the 'area of life' (house) it falls in, in your individual birthchart. Try to set this intention within 12 hours of the exact time of the New Moon for what you want to manifest in the coming month.

However, we can go even deeper here. If a New Moon falls within 3° of a planet in your chart, or one of the main horizontal or vertical axes, then there are potentially *two* areas of life where a new beginning may manifest. To understand this, we have to understand that each planet rules a sign, or in the case of Mercury and Venus, two signs. We have mentioned this earlier in the book with regard to the North Node and Midheaven.

Just refer back to the table on page 79 with the planetary symbols and the signs they rule. You will notice that Mercury rules two signs, Gemini and Virgo, and Venus rules two signs, Taurus and Libra. You can just keep this table as a reference when you are looking at your chart, or can even learn them off by heart. They are quite quick to learn, and then you have made your first step in learning astrology. These 'rulerships' are absolutely fundamental in astrology, I can't emphasise them enough. If you take your study further, they become vital in interpreting a birthchart fully.

Let's say your natal Mars is at 25° Taurus. If a New Moon falls 3° either side of your Mars (that is 22–28° Taurus), that means that you are likely to have a new beginning in the house where the New Moon falls in your chart, but also in the house which Mars rules in your chart, which will be the house with the Aries cusp.

In our example chart below Mars is at 7° Cancer, and it rules the 8th house (Aries is the 8th house cusp in this chart), so there may well be a new beginning in that area of life too. It's important to say that the closer the aspect between the New Moon and your natal planet, the more likely it is to manifest. A 3° orb either way would be the maximum. Occasionally a sign may be contained entirely within a house, or a sign may at times have two house cusps in it; this is all okay. It's normal for the houses to be of unequal sizes. It's to do with some very complex reasons of time and space, which we won't get into here, just accept that the chart you have is correct.

In our example chart Venus is at 4° Cancer. Therefore if we have a New Moon in our example chart falling at 1° Cancer, within 3° of Venus, Venus always has the general meaning of love, and money, so this person may have new beginnings in one or both areas. However, it is likely to also signal a new beginning not only in the house where the New Moon falls (10th house in our example chart), but also in the 2nd and the 9th houses, which Venus also rules in this example chart, via its rulership of both Taurus and Libra. Therefore she may have several new beginnings potentially manifesting at the same time, in the areas of career, money and long-distance travel; for example it could be an international business trip for a lucrative new contract. Work this process through for your own birthchart, as if a New Moon was falling on your Venus, and see which areas of life this would potentially affect. You may not always have all three areas manifesting, but certainly at least one area of life highlighted should be offering an opportunity for a new beginning of some kind.

To be clear: you are not going to be moving home or changing career every time you have a New Moon falling in certain parts of your chart, but these lunations do act as timing triggers for the larger planetary cycles. Then you start to become aware of any new opportunities appearing that you can

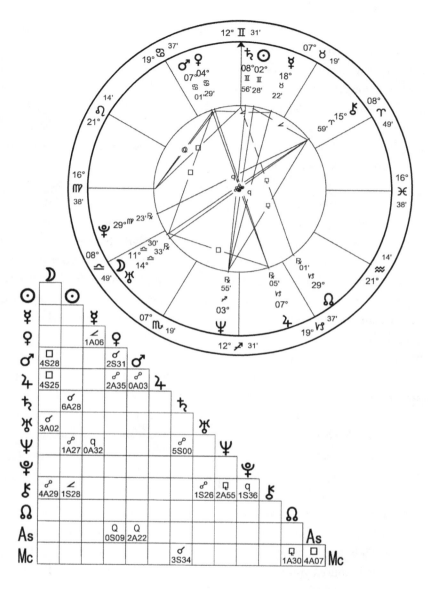

Astrological Calculations by Solar Fire software, Astrolabe Inc (www.alabe.com)

act on, as the new seed in that area of life manifests for you. Just watch for the signs, and you will start to see how your life unfolds.

There are several wonderful reasons for doing this. Firstly, you start to see that you are not living a random, meaningless life, *that there is a divine pattern unfolding that links you to the cosmos* with these monthly lunations.

147

We feel purposeless very often when we feel separate from the universe, that we are disconnected and have no role to play. These simple observations between your birthchart and the movements of the Moon increase your sense of connection to this divine intelligence and to planetary movements, and it becomes incredibly exciting. We start to notice the reliability of these measures too, and start to trust our birthchart as our guide. I would never suggest that our birthcharts should dictate to us; quite the contrary, I think this is useful information to enable us to become more empowered, with a much fuller understanding of who we really are. It also enables us to time opportunities better, instead of living life randomly.

The axes (Ascendant-Descendant, and Midheaven-IC) of your birthchart are highly sensitive points. Therefore if you have a New Moon falling within 3° of your Ascendant, it could suggest a new relationship, or a new step in your identity in how you project yourself to the world. Sometimes it can even suggest that you change your appearance in some way, or start to project yourself with much more confidence, depending on where the other planetary cycles are moving in your chart too.

Your Midheaven as discussed earlier is connected to your work, your career, your social status (for instance, married, single, divorced) and can indicate changes in those, and your reputation; but at a deeper level it is connected with your life path, where you are headed, and the values you want to stand for. It also represents one of the parents, usually the mother. The opposite end, the base of the vertical line, is the IC or 'Imum Coeli', meaning 'bottom of the sky', and it represents our early home life, our roots, and one of our parents; usually the father. So if you have a New Moon happening close to your IC, and you are looking to move home, this can often signal a trigger for things to move forward with that house move. If you are looking for a new job, and you have a New Moon happening close to your MC (or in your 10th house), you may find you get a job offer then, or actually begin a new job. Ideally you need the outer planetary cycles to be supporting these changes too, but I am consistently surprised after all these years how reliably these 'trigger points' of New Moons work in your chart and in your life. Just watch for a few months and see how they unfold. Sometimes they will bring about an event, but at other times it is just an idea, a meeting, or you deciding to begin a project that you had been putting off.

If New Moons represent new beginnings, Full Moons are cycles of completion, culmination or fruition. They often represent the results of our efforts. For instance, if falling in the 10th house of career, they may represent the end of a project we have been working on, or even the end of a job. Falling in the 9th house, they may represent the end of a long trip abroad, or the end of a period of study. Falling in the 7th house, they can at times represent the end of a relationship (although larger planetary cycles would also have to be involved), or they can indicate the relationship moving onto a different level, such as moving in with your partner. Full Moons can also shine a light on something that has remained hidden or secret up to now, and the discovery of that 'secret' can make you move in a different direction from that point onwards.

It's important to note that these New Moons and Full Moons are not the only indicators and timers of your development, by any means. At any one time you will have many transits and progressions from other planets, forming a complex matrix with your own birthchart. The planetary transits can all be followed in my video, newsletter and updates on social media (click on the Facebook icon on my website to follow my blog posts) and many of them will be very significant for you. However, they often require a great deal of astrological understanding, whereas the New Moons and Full Moons are happening every month, and everyone will be experiencing them. Lunations are also relatively easy to explain without involving you in detailed astrology, and it's easy for you to understand their meaning in your birthchart.

Eclipses are turbo-powered versions of the lunations. We can feel the influence of New Moons and Full Moons for up to two weeks either side of the exact date, whereas with Eclipses we can easily feel them up to a month before and at least six months afterwards, and they can be very powerful in their manifestation. Some astrologers believe that the effect of an Eclipse lasts as many years as the Eclipse lasts in hours, on average about three and a half hours (so three and a half years). However the closer they are to the exact date when they are happening, the more likely you are to see a manifestation of them in your life. Eclipses are portals when we can receive high level information from the cosmos more easily, and achieve a greater sense of connection both to the cosmos, and to our purpose in this lifetime. This is because they change the electromagnetic field of the Earth, and sensitive people particularly feel this. Again, the more exact they are to a planet or an angle (Ascendant or Midheaven axes), the more likely they are to produce an effect in your life.

Solar Eclipses are super-big New Moons, new beginnings, and can act like wild cards in your life. Things can come out of the blue, but are always relevant to the house (area of life) where the Eclipse falls, or if it aspects a planet, then also in the area of life that the planet rules. Watch how it unfolds in your own life. Sometimes a benefactor appears unexpectedly whom you barely know, who wants to support what you are doing, or help you in some way. Solar Eclipses can step change your life and catapult you forward in your destiny, and give you more prominence. They accelerate your development. If you have wandered from your path, Eclipses can bring you back onto it.

Eclipses can only happen close to the transiting Nodal Axis (within 12° for a Solar Eclipse, and 18° for a Lunar Eclipse), and therefore always have a sense of destiny about them, as the Nodal Axis moving through the heavens is connected to our *collective* destiny. However, if they fall close to your own *natal* North Node, your personal line of destiny, it can be particularly powerful. You can get more insights and clarity about what you are meant to be doing in this life, with an even greater sense of purpose. A Lunar Eclipse has a similar effect, but with more of a sense of completion, and often a change in direction from that point. It can clearly mark the end or culmination of work projects, jobs and relationships, but only when that is appropriate for your development. Lunar Eclipses can often bring up a lot of emotion, as they are super-big Full Moons and can signify endings, but with a sense of releasing the old that no longer serves you. Focus on releasing the old and surrendering to the new at any Full Moon or Lunar Eclipse.

Eclipses can therefore bring major life change, especially when they fall close to a natal planet or angle. They act like reset buttons, and often produce a feeling of events speeding up. They are likely to bring change in the areas of your birthchart where they fall. Eclipses occur in opposing signs for around 18 months; so for instance from May 2017 to November 2018 they will be moving through Leo and its opposing sign, Aquarius. See where those signs fall in your chart, as they are likely to be areas of activity, change and development in your life over that period. For me, these are falling in my 3rd house of writing (Aquarius) and my 9th house of publishing (Leo), which is why I am choosing to write this book now. Then after November 2018 the Eclipses will start to move into Cancer and Capricorn, as the Nodal Axis continually shifts. A list of Eclipses up to the end of 2020 is at the end of this chapter for you, so you can follow these in your own birthchart and your own life. Just observe what happens in these areas of your life that are activated by these Eclipses, and feel that you are experiencing a direct connection with the cosmos in doing this.

Another important thing to note is that there tends to be a continuing theme while the Eclipses are occurring in the same sign; that is they will advance the theme in your life that began with the first Eclipse in the series in, for instance, Leo and Aquarius. So you learn to be very observant, conscious and aware of your unfolding development and opportunities.

When a lunation falls on a planet in your birthchart that will also have the generalised meaning of the planets themselves. Those meanings are likely to manifest too, so you may well have several potential meanings happening for any lunation, in different areas of life. These definitions below are by necessity general, as they are not defined within a particular sign or house that you will be able to work out in your own birthchart, but will still be helpful for you in understanding the symbolism. Remember that a New Moon or Full Moon may be fleeting in its effect, a couple of weeks to either side of the exact date, but an Eclipse will be more powerful and long-lasting. If the ruling planet of your Ascendant or Midheaven is aspected, this will be particularly important for you. Remember also that the rulerships of the houses are incredibly important in astrology. Therefore the meanings of any lunation may become multi-layered for you.

Always remember that the general meaning of these planets is modified by the sign and house in which they fall. The most important thing is where the lunations fall by 'house', and then whether they aspect a planet, which will bring other areas of life into the picture for you, indicated by the house(s) that this aspected planet rules.

Now we're going to go through the general meaning of the planets, so you can anticipate how lunations coming together with these planets may work for you. It can feel like you are briefly 'blended' with the symbolism of the planet when a lunation is conjunct it.

The list below details lunations coming to conjunct the following planets:

Your Natal Sun – the Sun rules Leo

Your Sun represents how your energy is expressed; note if it is in a fire sign (Aries, Leo, Sagittarius), when your energy is likely to express in a fiery way; in an Earth sign (Taurus, Virgo, Capricorn), when it is likely to express in

151

a more down-to-earth, practical, reliable way; in an air sign (Gemini, Libra, Aquarius), when it is likely to express in a sociable or intellectual way; or in a water sign (Cancer, Scorpio, Pisces), when it is likely to express in a feeling, emotional, sensitive way.

Your Sun is also related to things that bring you joy, and where you feel your passion, and you are uplifted. A Solar Eclipse can bring in new opportunities where you get noticed in a more public way, you 'shine' in front of others, and there is a greater degree of recognition. A New Moon or Solar Eclipse can bring a sense of play and vitality to you, whereas a Lunar Eclipse may briefly make you feel a little depleted energetically. It can appear to 'Eclipse' your energy, while it is actually rebooting it to take you in a slightly different direction. It's almost comical, but my Sun is in Pisces, the sign of the fish, and twice in my life when Lunar Eclipses have come together with my Sun I have been very ill for 24 hours as a result of eating fish! The universe does seem to have a very literal sense of humour sometimes.

Your Natal Moon – the Moon rules Cancer

Your Moon is your instinctive reaction to things; it operates on a very deep level. It can represent your home, your mother, the women in your life, your own sense of motherhood (so can be linked to birth issues), hormones and your own sense of security and deep connectedness in the world. If you have your birthchart Moon in the 5th house, and want children, when you have a New Moon or Solar Eclipse coming to 'conjunct' your natal Moon, then it can suggest a pregnancy. A Lunar Eclipse here may suggest the end of the pregnancy.

The Moon is very sensitive, and rules the stomach and the breasts.

Your Natal Mercury – rules Gemini and Virgo

Your Mercury is connected to your mind, your thinking processes, your 'mindset', how your mind perceives things, and your communication. The sign it is in will determine whether that is logical, deep thinking, or skittish and has trouble focusing. Mercury has a natural affinity with the 3rd house in the chart (because of its rulership of Gemini, the third sign), and therefore is also linked to paperwork, correspondence, transport, technology, and agreements and contracts of various kinds. Mercury is also connected to youth, siblings and neighbours. Mercury rules the hands, the lungs and the nervous system.

So a New Moon or Solar Eclipse may bring in new ideas for you, for instance new plans that you want to communicate; or it may be linked to some important documentation that moves you forward in your life. I have known people buy a new car when they have a 'new beginning' aspecting their Mercury, as it rules transport. A Lunar Eclipse may mean your difficult neighbour moves away, or there is some 'closure' with a friend or sibling.

Your Natal Venus – rules Taurus and Libra

Your natal Venus symbolises love, and also creature comforts and money. In its rulership of Taurus, Venus may enjoy the good things in life, beautiful material objects, and good food and solid resources. Libra is linked to the arts and culture, and again, beautiful things. Venus is about pleasure, and so is linked to having a happy social time. For a man, Venus can symbolise the woman in his life. Venus also rules the throat, neck and thyroid (Taurus connections), and via Libra the pancreas and spleen, and release of insulin (Venus can be overindulgent and enjoy the sweet things of life, in all senses).

A New Moon or Solar Eclipse to your Venus may bring a new relationship into your life, and even make us more attractive or charming. It may bring in a new source of income, if the other transits support this. It may simply be an opportunity to enjoy the arts more, or be particularly social.

A Full Moon or Lunar Eclipse can suggest a culmination in any of these areas (for instance you hold an art exhibition) which is the result of your efforts, or may even see the ending of a relationship, if that is no longer appropriate for your development.

Your Natal Mars – rules Aries

Your natal Mars is connected to your energy, your assertiveness, and your get-up-and-go. If your Mars is in a fire sign (Aries, Leo, Sagittarius), you are likely to have a lot of physical energy, enthusiasm and radiance for life. Mars is linked to the athlete, the pioneer, going solo, being high achieving, setting goals, and how 'driven' and 'type A' high achieving a personality you are, and this will be modified by the sign and house it is in in your birthchart. Mars in Pisces will assert her/himself very gently and sensitively, whereas Mars in Aries is much more of a 'warrior' in all that he or she does, and instinctively has a lot of fight in him/her. Mars can be linked to impatience and being impetuous too, if it is in a fire sign in your chart.

In a woman's chart, Mars can represent the type of man she is looking for in her life.

Mars is linked to the head, men in general, athletes, soldiers and surgeons, and also to blood and adrenaline.

A New Moon or Solar Eclipse if you are female may represent a new man in your life, or beginning a new 'fight' for something, a new cause. It can also be new physical activity, such as beginning a new sport or a new physical regime.

A Full Moon or Lunar Eclipse may suggest a culmination of a sporting event, or something at which you have been working very hard. It can even suggest a slowdown in your energy as a result of your efforts.

Your Natal Jupiter – rules Sagittarius

Your natal Jupiter represents expansion, personal growth, abundance, wisdom, learning, self-improvement, optimism, higher education, writing and teaching, publishing, long-distance travel, the law, religion and philosophy, and big visions that you may aspire to. It is connected to spiritual growth, higher consciousness, and honours; recognition at a high level. It is associated with a reaching out, a desire to expand your knowledge and experience. Jupiter is associated also with humour, spontaneity, adventure, exploring, being an opportunist and a visionary. It tends to be future-oriented, and can always see bigger and better opportunities for self and others. Wherever it falls in your birthchart, there is often a sense of protection or being lucky. The word 'jovial' is associated with Jupiter; it is big-hearted and generous.

Physically, it is linked to the sciatic nerve, the liver, the detoxification process, and the thighs. It has a tendency (linked to expansion) of overindulgence.

A New Moon or Solar Eclipse coming to your Jupiter can bring new travel or training/education experiences, or a desire to improve oneself in some way. There can be a desire to teach, to write and to publish; to expand your profile in the world. They can bring very positive recognition to you, personal growth opportunities, and abundance. You may see a situation differently, via a shift in your consciousness, and this gives you a more positive vision for the future.

A Full Moon or Lunar Eclipse can signify the end of a big trip abroad, or of a period of study or professional exams. It can be the pinnacle of a period of self-improvement (so see which house it is in in your birthchart, and which house it rules, for more information). It can shine a light on your success, and make you even better recognised for what you do. It may even bring money in for you.

Your Natal Saturn – rules Capricorn

Your natal Saturn represents your father, how you handle responsibility, your discipline, and the way your life is structured. It is naturally associated with the 10th house, so it is linked to your reputation, your career, and how hard you have worked to achieve professional status. It is linked to how able you are to deal with practical matters, be organised, and if we play by the rules and work hard Saturn will offer us hard-won success. If Jupiter is jovial, Saturn is serious, and gets on with the job at hand. There is an appreciation of tradition and structured hierarchies, so someone with a strong Saturn may be able to work with or for organisations such as government or big businesses. Saturn gives you the discipline to hang in for the long term to achieve what you want.

Saturn is linked to Chronos, Lord of Time (think chronology), so I think of Saturn as a 3D planet which is associated with density (materials such as lead) and tangible objects. It rules teeth, bones and skin in the body, and the skeletal structure in general. Because of its link to chronology, it is also associated with age, older people and patience.

A New Moon or Solar Eclipse to your natal Saturn could suggest some new beginning with your work, or the beginning of some project that could involve a lot of dedication, effort and patience. It may involve some shift in your reputation or status too.

A Full Moon or Lunar Eclipse may suggest some issue around your father, or an older relative, or the end of a project at work, or even your job or career. It can be the culmination of much effort, where you reap the rewards but still have much responsibility. It may shine a light on some issue at work, or with your father, of which you may have been unaware.

Your Natal Uranus – rules Aquarius

Uranus, Neptune and Pluto move much more slowly than the planets we have already looked at, and therefore people of approximately the same age are going to be experiencing the Eclipses to these planets at the same time as you. They are still equally powerful, especially in terms of the houses in your birthchart that these planets rule. These are likely to be different even amongst people of similar ages, as the clock face of your birthchart is determined not only by your date and place of birth, but also by your precise birthtime.

Uranus is linked to your individual self-expression, your independence, your freedom and your originality. Its energy is intense, often bringing with it a feeling of urgency. When it is aspected it can also suggest a change in geography which will give you more freedom of self-expression, or help you redefine your individuality in a new context. It can certainly bring change, for it is the planet of fast-moving, often unexpected change in your life. It is connected to superconscious perception and brilliant insights, so they may be part of the picture too. Uranus rules the ankles and circulation.

A New Moon or Solar Eclipse to your Uranus can suggest that there will be exciting times ahead, and it is likely to bring unexpected change to you. As Uranus is the 'outsider', and rules unusual people, you may find that people who have a different background to you come into your life; they may be younger, or have a different nationality and social background. They may feel exciting or unusual compared to the people you normally meet. You are likely to feel restless for change at this time, and this could include a change of geography, or even a change in your work so more of your creative self-expression can come through. If you are a woman, often a male figure appears in your life who may well be foreign, although there is likely to be an erratic quality to the relationship.

A Full Moon or Lunar Eclipse can suggest that your restlessness with the 'status quo' is reaching a peak, and you must make some radical changes. It can indicate a strong desire for more variety and freedom in your life, to go places and do things that you have never done before, and this feeling can be urgent and irresistible. Change has to happen after this to satisfy these feelings, and be prepared to be flexible.

Your Natal Neptune – rules Pisces

Neptune is associated with creativity, spirituality and a fine perception; a highlighted Neptune in your chart means that you may be tuned into intangibles, perhaps seeing or feeling energy, or knowing how people are feeling beneath their words. It is linked to inspiration, imagination, dreams, healing, miracles, consciousness and bliss. Creatively, it is linked to a fine perception, which can express in various art forms and even in photography or film. I feel that Neptune is associated with fifth-dimensional reality, outside time and space; those times when we are 'lost in a dream' or our creativity are when we are expressing our Neptune. It is connected to 'altered states'.

The less positive side of Neptune is when this 'dreaminess' starts to express as confusion, or no longer knowing where you are going and what you are doing, you can feel in a fog. It can suggest deception or disappointment or 'things not being as they seem'. Neptune is also linked to addiction such as drugs or alcohol as they create an altered state. Neptune can have an 'undertow' effect on your confidence too; the key thing if you are starting to express the negative side of Neptune is to do something creative or spiritual, such as meditation, for it then uses up the energy positively so it is less able to manifest negatively. The music has to play somehow, so much better to make sure it plays positively.

Neptune rules the feet, the lymphatic system, and the immune system.

A New Moon or Solar Eclipse to your Neptune could bring a new creative project, or an urge to start to incorporate a spiritual practice into your life; you may feel that you want to get more involved in charity work, to help people, or even healing work. It may be the beginning of film or photographic work, or the beginning of learning how to sail (Neptune in myth is Lord of the Sea), or going on a sea trip. You may feel that your energy is becoming more refined, and can sense things at a subtle level more easily. Your dreams may become more important, and you may want to become more reclusive for a while in order to go within yourself. It may initiate a spiritual experience.

A Full Moon or Lunar Eclipse in general can mean that something is revealed that you were unaware of, but this is even more the case if either of them falls on your Neptune; this is because Neptune rules secrets, and 'things not being as they seem'. So this can result in your disappointment or disillusionment, and therefore you change your course of action going forward. It may be that you become aware of the addiction of someone close to you, or your own addiction reaches a point where you have to make some changes.

Neptune is connected to allergies and leaky gut, so there may be revelations that help you understand this condition and what may heal you.

Your Natal Pluto – rules Scorpio

Pluto is the planet of power, sex, death and transformation, and rather like Uranus, its energy can feel intense, in a deep, fundamental way. It often brings up the past, in order for any old repressed energy to be released. People from the past may reappear, and there is often a feeling of fatedness around Pluto. Any aspects to Pluto can trigger power struggles, manipulation, control, intensity and compulsion in relationships. The urge to get involved with people may be irresistible, even if you know it may not be a smooth, calm relationship. It can bring up compulsive behaviour patterns too.

Pluto works beneath the surface, so there is often a feeling of powerful emotions and urges driving your behaviour, but the purpose is always to bring psychological patterns to consciousness so you can transform them and empower yourself.

Pluto also rules taxes, investments, insurances, inheritance and joint finance, so when aspected these areas of life may come into prominence. Often it is linked to permanent separation, so there can even be a death of someone close to you, indicated by the area of the chart associated with your Pluto.

Pluto rules the reproductive system, and elimination from the body.

A New Moon or Solar Eclipse to your Pluto may bring in a new intense relationship, which can be highly sexual, or it can bring power issues to the fore in your workplace. You may begin a new project to regenerate or refurbish something, or even begin some in-depth psychological work on yourself. An aspect to Pluto can bring permanent changes to your life, but they do not necessarily happen quickly. Often, a New Moon or Solar Eclipse can give you a stronger sense of your own power.

A Full Moon or Lunar Eclipse can reveal secrets that you were unaware of, as Pluto in its rulership of Scorpio rules secrets and cover-ups. They may be of a sexual or a financial nature. Equally you may begin to notice old behaviour patterns that no longer serve you coming to the fore, or you are consciously working on any old blocked energy or resentment that is stopping you moving forward. It can often be a time when you finally see the results of a project in which you have invested a great deal of energy and effort, and which has taken time. This is often a powerful time of fundamental change in your life that may involve separations from people.

If an Eclipse conjuncts any planet in your birthchart, it sensitises it for the next six months, and so if another planet such as the Sun, Venus, Mars or Jupiter passes over that Eclipse degree point, it may again be activated. So whatever began at the Eclipse for you may be highlighted as the Sun passes over it; beauty or love may be brought into the picture as Venus passes, then energised as Mars passes, and expanded as Jupiter passes, often with success or abundance manifesting.

The most powerful aspect with lunations is when a New or Full Moon, or especially an Eclipse, comes to conjunct an angle (either end of the axes) in the birthchart: so that is the Ascendant (identity and relationship), Descendant (relationship), Midheaven (career, life path, status), and the IC (your roots, your home; could also represent a change with a parent). As with every aspect in astrology, the more exactly the lunations conjunct your planets or angles, the more likely they are to manifest. If you are going through a couple of months when you have almost every lunation aspecting planets and angles in your chart, that will represent a particularly busy period of time for you.

Although it is helpful to be aware of the larger planetary cycles and where they are moving through your birthchart, even watching these lunations is very powerful, as you start to see the precise symbolism manifesting in your chart and in your life. This is your soul unfolding in its development, as it was destined to do from the 'acorn' that is your chart. The pattern and timing was set at your birth. That's always amazing to me to ponder upon.

What is important when you are watching these lunations unfold in your life is to **always see them in the context of your Nodal Axis and Midheaven,** that is your 'big picture', your path of destiny and how you are likely to express it in the world. The Eclipses are bigger aspects than the New and Full Moons, but even the New and Full Moons create stepping stones along our journey to become who are meant to become in this lifetime. Each of them represents a trigger to jump us forward in our destiny.

This chapter has given you the tools so that you can start to work with the Moon's cycles to maximise your potential at any given moment. You now understand the importance of lunations, and particularly Eclipses, in your development. As the months go by you can start to anticipate what might be unfolding for you, as you now know which houses they will be falling in in your birthchart, and also whether they will be aspecting any other planets or angles in your birthchart (Ascendant/Descendant/Midheaven/IC).

Here is a list of the Eclipses running up to 2020. I will be talking about each of these in more detail in my YouTube videos, monthly newsletters and social media posts.

Upcoming Eclipses to 2020

Eclipses, as we have noted earlier, are powerful 'pivot points' in your life, and it is important to see in which areas of your birthchart they are falling. Eclipses form in pairs, so through any 18-month period we will see them alternating between opposite signs, for instance Leo and Aquarius up to November 2018, when they will move into Cancer and Capricorn. The houses where they fall in your birthchart will mark areas of activity and change for you in those areas of life, so they are well worth observing. Then follow what we set out previously in terms of guidelines of interpretation.

As Eclipses alter the electromagnetic field of the Earth, they offer us particular timings to make leaps in our evolution. Plan to benefit from them by using the methods we have recommended in this book, to live your North Node potential to a higher and higher level. They provide outstanding development opportunities, as they accelerate our personal evolution. All of this moves us from victim consciousness to the magnificent co-creators we are meant to become.

The table below shows the upcoming Eclipses up to the end of 2020. They are expressed as degrees and minutes of a sign. For instance, 15° Aquarius 25.

Lunar	7th August 2017	15° Aquarius 25
Solar (Total)	21st August 2017	28° Leo 53
Lunar	31st January 2018	11° Leo 37
Solar	15th February 2018	27° Aquarius 08
Solar	13th July 2018	20° Cancer 41
Lunar	27th July 2018	04° Aquarius 45
Solar	11th August 2018	18° Leo 42
Solar	6th January 2019	15° Capricorn 25

Lunar	21st January 2019	00° Leo 52
Solar	2nd July 2019	10° Cancer 37
Lunar	16th July 2019	24° Capricorn 04
Solar	26th December 2019	4° Capricorn 07
Lunar	10th January 2020	20° Cancer 00
Lunar	5th June 2020	15° Sagittarius 34
Solar	21st June 2020	00° Cancer 21
Lunar	5th July 2020	13° Capricorn 38
Lunar	30th November 2020	08° Gemini 38
Solar	14th December 2020	23° Sagittarius 08

On a personal note, I began writing this book at the Solar Eclipse of 1st September 2016, when this 'new beginning' Eclipse was close to my Midheaven of career. It will be published as the Lunar Eclipse (representing culminations/endings) on the 7th August 2017 at 15° Aquarius comes to fall on my North Node in the 3rd house of writing, and the Solar Eclipse (new beginnings) on 21st August 2017 at 29° Leo falls in my 9th house of publishing. These months of writing and researching have taken me on a profound personal journey.

They have taken me far deeper into my own self than I ever imagined at the start of this project, and made me understand through revelations in dreams and meditations how rich the symbolism of the Nodal Axis is, and how powerful Eclipses can be as turning points in our understanding. I have glimpsed layers and layers of meaning connected to my South Node, which act as fuel for my soul's evolution in this life. There appear to have been many lifetimes on the same 'soul theme', and there have been dazzling synchronicities linked to my Nodal Axis all the way through writing this book. It's as if in giving my attention to this profound aspect of my chart, it has been illuminated. This has been fascinating, and I feel as if my life has been thrown into high relief; so even though I was already on the correct path in living my Nodal Axis, it now has such height and depth that goes far beyond the simple descriptions in this book, and yet fully reflects them. That's why I believe it takes some of your own effort and alchemy to explore what may appear to be deceptively simple statements, to find that you are, as Dr John Dee would describe, turning your lead into gold and transmuting yourself to a higher level of being.

That is my wish for you all.

9 Power Period 2017–2020

We are now entering a very powerful period in the world running up to 2020, and some of this change is signified by the Eclipses. In this chapter, I'm outlining some of the broad trends running up to 2020. If you would like a much more detailed look at how world events and trends are likely to be unfolding up to 2020, there is a comprehensive new chapter covering these at the end of the second edition of *You Don't Really Believe in Astrology, Do You?*

2017 is operating as the setup year for these major changes, partly indicated by the opposition between Jupiter and Uranus. This aspect between Jupiter and Uranus through 2017 is exciting, empowering and idealistic. Jupiter represents higher consciousness, and Uranus is the planet linked to awakening, the superconscious and the 'Mind of God'. So there are likely to be more and more people 'waking up' and wanting a better way to live; a soaring vision of a new society that has at its core mutual respect for all. It can offer us rapid shifts in perception and possibility, so that we can see bigger horizons for ourselves and the world than we ever could before. It encourages innovation, new thinking and new technology. As we shift our frequency, other possibilities become accessible that we may have been unaware of before. So 2017 is fast-moving, at times volatile and turbulent, as we start to see the questioning of long-standing institutions, but it feels tremendously exciting and empowering for us as individuals if we can use our astrology to help us ride the waves. This aspect can take us beyond a gradual progression in our development to quantum leaps in our evolution, even developing new faculties that were previously unavailable to us.

What may help to boost this evolution is the semi-square between Uranus and Neptune, which broadly is in effect from now until mid-2019. Neptune represents the spiritual, the mystical, a sense of oneness with All That Is, and altered states. It is also connected to healing and light. Uranus can offer us sudden jumps in insight and understanding (which are expanded when it is opposed by Jupiter in 2017), but is also the planet most linked to technology. Therefore this aspect can be about 'inspired technology' that can help to shift us to those altered states by the use of new devices. For example, the amount of 'light' we have in our bodies can be boosted by laser watches; such devices already exist, and these and light therapy healing are likely to become very common.

Neptune is in Pisces, the sign it rules, until 2025; it is linked to the ethereal, spiritual, mystical side of life. Therefore with this Uranus-Neptune aspect it is likely that abilities such as channelling and telepathy are likely to be helped by new devices, and will become the 'new normal'. This may be particularly the case for those born under the conjunction of Uranus and Neptune from January 1991 to December 1995. This technology that will help to facilitate our shift in frequency will certainly aid our ability to create our own reality more easily. It can accelerate the process. Other innovations are discussed later in this chapter.

Another area where we may expect to see much more development is evidence of life beyond this Earth. This will start from 2017 onwards, and is likely to increase over the coming years.

One of the most intense events during this period is the total Solar Eclipse of 21st August 2017. The path of this Eclipse falls west to east across America, and therefore the US is likely to be the focus for manifestations of this Eclipse, as that is how they have historically worked. The Solar Eclipse is at 28° 53 Leo, and interestingly it falls almost exactly on the US president's Ascendant, and his Mars. It is also conjunct the Royal Star Regulus, symbol of the King (which the president has natally on his Ascendant), and Regulus also has military connotations. It is possible therefore that there could be conflict of some kind, or a threat of conflict, or there could be some major constitutional issue as Mars in the president's chart rules his 9th house of legal and constitutional matters.

The years up to and including 2020 will be a very intense time of transformation for the world, a shift from the old paradigm of the patriarchy and corporatism into a new world where society becomes more horizontal and less vertical in its organisation. We will ultimately be less answerable to external, controlling authorities. 2020 is likely to be a peak year in this change, and we are likely to see much polarisation in the world as people become aware that the old ways of thinking and operating are no longer working.

The shift of Jupiter and Saturn into Aquarius in December 2020, a very important social cycle, later followed by Pluto moving into Aquarius in 2024, sends us a clear message to be authentic and live our own truth. Become aligned to your values, walk your talk, and the closer your day-to-day life is to your true essence, the better your life will work. Start living like this now. Become a campaigner, a trailblazer, a visionary, shining a light on a better vision of a better world. More and more of you will be moving from making a living to making a real contribution to society, and astrology can be your compass by following the vision of your North Node.

This move of Jupiter and Saturn into air signs (Aquarius) is the first time in almost 600 years. In combination they are connected to social structures. Up to December 2020, this conjunction of Jupiter and Saturn has occurred in Earth signs since 1842. When we think of Earth we think of density, permanence and permanent ownership, material and practical security, and slowness. Our societies have been defined by these qualities. When we think of Air, we think of lightness, flexibility, impermanence, and speed. The element of Air is connected to our mental function, and so information exchange is likely to become even faster. Transport will be speeded up, particularly aeronautics, as Aquarius is ruled by Uranus, the planet most associated with aviation. There will be a revolution in transport, for instance Uber is planning to test a flying car by 2020, there is already talk of parcels being delivered by drones, and in 2018 China plans to introduce the 'trackless train' that runs on virtual rails.

From now on we are likely to see society becoming more digitised and electronically based, and even more so from December 2020 when Jupiter and Saturn move into Aquarius, which is the sign linked to technology, electronics and electrics. Electric cars will become much more common, and that will help reduce pollution in cities. Flying cars, if they are introduced widely, will reduce road traffic congestion enormously. As Aquarius is linked to freedom, having permanent home and car ownership may also become less common, as we start to value experiences and information over solidity and permanence.

Technology will advance in leaps and bounds, so we can imagine that we may simply summon an electric car to our current position via our smartphone, and that will take us to our destination. There will be a major shift in job structures as robots are able to take over more repetitive functions, and this will cause significant social changes; this will become a key question for governments.

As Uranus (connected to electrical energy and technology) moves into Taurus (the sign most associated with the human body) in May 2018 for seven years, we may see more technology applied to the body. This can be anywhere from smartwatches to chips that are implanted in us to track various body functions and regulate them; such a device already exists to regulate insulin. There will be personal vibrational energy devices that can restore us to good health; these already exist but will become more widespread. Smart devices will abound that can diagnose your physical condition within minutes, without the need for invasive testing. One is being introduced that is an app for your smartphone that can diagnose eye conditions, including potential blindness. This demonstrates another aspect of the Jupiter-Saturn shift into Aquarius, which is that increasingly healing will be vibrationally based, rather than via pharmaceuticals. This may accelerate the demise of the pharmaceutical companies. There will be widespread recognition that we are electrical, vibrational beings, before we are chemical beings. Lynne McTaggart expresses it well: "At our most elemental, we are not a chemical reaction, but an energetic charge. Human beings and all living things are a coalescence of energy in a field of energy connected to every other thing in the world. This pulsating energy field is the central engine of our being and our consciousness, the alpha and the omega of our existence." Lynne's view is likely to become much more widespread in the coming years.

There are likely to be big changes in the 'structures' of society over the next three years and beyond, as permanence and solidity is challenged with the shift of the Jupiter-Saturn conjunction from Earth to Air. These include governments, banks, big corporations and financial institutions, particularly those that have not acted with integrity. 2020 will be the crunch year of accountability and consequent crumbling where any corruption is involved.

The themes building up to 2020 have already begun; 2017 will be a year of social activism and idealism, with the opposition between Jupiter and Uranus, and with more and more people feeling that there is a better way to live than via the control of autocratic and external authority. The square between Uranus in Aries and Pluto in Capricorn from 2012 to 2017 has seen the build-up around independence and freedom, with many challenging the powerful institutions of the status quo (Pluto in Capricorn). There is likely to be more and more polarisation of control versus freedom until we reach a peak in 2020. There will be a move towards a decentralised peer-to-peer society where people try to operate beyond current social controls.

As Uranus moves into Taurus in May 2018, and Taurus is also connected to banking, we are likely to see a revolution in that area too, involving technology. This won't simply be the ability to do all of our banking from our smartphones. Increasingly we will be moving to a digital, cashless society. Many countries are moving in that direction, and Australia, India and Sweden are ahead of the pack here. Soon we won't even need a password; our identity will be checked via a thumbprint or retina scan. It is highly likely that cash will disappear in an increasingly digitised economy.

As we move towards 2020, more and more of us will endeavour to become more self-sufficient, such as growing some of our own food, and becoming more community-based as we all come together to help each other. Ultimately from 2021 onwards there will be a greater sense of society being based on collectives, people living in communities with other people who share similar values, rather than in our current vertically structured societies. This is suggested by the move of Jupiter and Saturn into Aquarius in December 2020. So we may be moving geographically to live in communities of like-minded people, or at a minimum forming a 'tribe' with them via social media, also linked to Aquarius. The control of governments and corporations is very likely to be reduced, and innovative solutions to problems will grow from the grass roots upwards; this is suggested by the positive aspect (trine) of self-sufficiency between Saturn and Uranus through 2017.

Increasingly, many of us will become concerned about issues of pollution and toxicity, whether from pesticides or electromagnetic frequencies, and the Uranus-Neptune aspect can also encourage the development of devices that neutralise (Neptune = dissolve) harmful electromagnetic frequencies (Uranus) from Wi-Fi, smart meters, and cell phones. There will be increased technology to clean up the Earth, but also many people wanting to live a simpler life in harmony with the Earth. Another side of this Uranus-Neptune aspect is the shift to cleaner energy, such as wind and solar. There will undoubtedly be big challenges to heavy industry, oil and fossil fuels in general as we move towards 2020. The shift of Jupiter into Scorpio in October 2017 until November 2018 could begin this process of recycling and detoxifying.

The move of Uranus into Taurus in May 2018 is likely to have a polarising effect; on the one hand, the Earth (Taurus) will become increasingly electrified, with even more electromagnetic radiation from Wi-Fi and other devices. These interfere with the Earth's natural frequency. On the other hand, the power of the electromagnetic frequency of the Earth as a healing energy will become more fully recognised, and some people may even move to areas where this energy is particularly concentrated. The transit of Uranus through Taurus from 2018 to 2025 may also witness an increasing interest in organic farming and natural methods of production, benefitting from the Earth's natural healing frequency, as Taurus is linked to the Earth, our natural resources, and agriculture.

There are already some wonderful developments in this area, and the generation born in the 1990s is highly environmentally and ecologically aware. They will birth many of our environmental solutions, and the ideas are likely to come from the grass roots upwards in terms of innovation (Uranus in Taurus). For instance, eco-villages are being developed in the Netherlands that will initially be introduced to Sweden, Denmark, Germany and Norway. Through the use of technology (Uranus) they are entirely self-sustaining (Taurus), producing healthy organic food from 'vertical farming' and using different light colours to produce the best growth in fruit and vegetables. This reflects not only Uranus in Taurus but Uranus in aspect to Neptune. The residents will all live off-grid, and produce not only their own energy but all their own clean food and water. It has been described as the 'Tesla of eco-villages'. There will be many more of these developments to come.

Already there are some inspired villages where the houses are easy to assemble, all supplied with solar power, and all the roofs are covered with organic vegetable gardens. These not only insulate the house, but also provide food. The houses are built in polymer sections which have water channels in them, making irrigation simple.

Energy will become free and clean. As well as solar-powered roof tiles we now have the smartflower™, which is a device that stands in your garden and can provide electricity for a family of four. It opens out in the sun like a flower, and folds up in rain or wind; that simple. Devices such as this will revolutionise the energy market.

As well as technological developments, there will be a rise of the 'divine feminine' over these years; a greater focus on feminine values, whatever gender you are. These are the values of love, co-operation, nurturing and protecting. It moves the focus from self to the care of others, the idea that everyone is equal and worthy of support and protection by society. There are many astrological indicators of this, and the growth of these values is likely to be in reaction to the dominant controlling patriarchy in society, with its values of capitalism, materialism, external authority and control.

This is suggested by several astrological aspects. Firstly, Venus the goddess of love and peace began its new (synodic) cycle in March 2017, in the sign of Aries. We could consider this the aspect of the 'warrior goddess'. Secondly, the dwarf planet Eris is in a powerful position, also in Aries, and conjunct Uranus until May 2018. Eris in myth is also the 'spiritual warrior', the sister of Mars (god of war), and fights against any oppression or injustice. Like Uranus, it challenges the establishment, and sees no limits. Its momentum is always in line with higher spiritual law, and is linked to an inner transformational journey. Eris is a radical, a maverick, and like Uranus is also an awakener of consciousness. In myth she fights against any corruption or lack of integrity, suggesting challenges to governments and corporations that have not behaved well. Again this suggests a considerable breakdown of these structures over the next few years, as Eris is also known as the great disruptor. As part of the symbolism of Eris there is a desire to control and punish the greed and excesses of a small section of society that has great influence on the rest. Eris is also linked to the birth of new ideas and concepts that will replace old, outmoded structures and ways of thinking. Eris was discovered in January 2005.

Then we have another dwarf planet Haumea, discovered in December 2004, just a month before Eris. This suggests that the combination of these two planets are going to be very powerful in our collective consciousness. Like Eris, Haumea also represents the feminine, as in myth she is linked to the Hawaiian goddess of childbirth and fertility. She acts in line with the essence of the natural world, and flows with it.

Whenever a planet is discovered and comes into strong aspects with others in the heavens, its symbolism, which is always derived from myth, becomes prominent in the world and becomes part of our consciousness. Examples in the past are when Uranus was discovered in 1781: it was the beginning of the American and French Revolutions, and Uranus is the planet of revolution. When Neptune, planet of altered states was discovered in 1846, that year was the beginning of the Spiritualist movement in New York State, which spread across the world. More recently in 1979, the asteroid Chiron was discovered, with the symbolism of the 'wounded healer', and very much linked to alternative medicine. Since that time, chiropractic (Chiron) treatments have become mainstream, as have many alternative therapies. Therefore the symbolism of Eris and Haumea are likely to become important in our consciousness now. Not only will feminine values of peace, love, nurturing, protecting, and co-operation become more evident, but particularly concern for the Earth, as that is linked to Haumea's symbolism. Both Eris and Haumea encourage a move to a world of sacredness and oneness.

Haumea has a long 285-year orbit, and at the moment her symbolism is coming to the fore as she is in a powerful aspect with four other planets. In 2017 she is in conjunction with Jupiter, opposing Uranus and Eris in Aries, and squaring Pluto in Capricorn. All of this symbolism speaks to greater equality and fairness in society, against capitalism, materialism and the patriarchy. In myth Haumea has the ability to not only protect but also regenerate the Earth after damage has been done by any toxicity and pollution. She sees the Earth as an organic, holistic, living body. Haumea has a magical, ethereal, Merlin-like quality. Haumea will always fight against the destructive use of power against nature, and supports, nurtures and protects the wild, instinctive world to be as divine intelligence intended it. She is linked to the sacredness of all life, the wisdom of the Earth and its primordial creative power, and the healing energy of plants and herbs.

In myth Haumea has a magic stick called Makalei by which she can summon seafood and produce wild food when mass agriculture has failed, due to toxicity and damage by pesticides and herbicides. Most importantly, the ancient Hawaiians were astronomers, ahead of their time, and believed that the world was made of vibrating energy, just as we have been describing here. In myth, Haumea believed that through our intentions and beliefs we can create new realities. So this recently discovered planet that has started to come to prominence because of its aspects to other planets in 2017 is absolutely right for the time, and for the theme of this book. Haumea was able to shape-shift in quantum reality, and therefore will aid our ability to use this understanding in our own lives. She is linked to the new consciousness.

This also suggests that our concern for the Earth and its sustainability and repair will come increasingly to the fore, and we will have the ability to restore its fertility and health in some way. For those who wish to do so, they will live more in harmony with the Earth, her simple natural rhythms, and better understand her power. Many of us will want to live closer to the Earth, as part of nature without interfering with it, and away from cities. The combination of the background of the Uranus-Pluto square, representing personal transformation and breakthrough, the Jupiter-Uranus opposition through 2017 of soaring new visions, horizons and possibilities, and maximising your potential at any moment, and the opposition of Haumea (quantum reality) to Uranus and Eris in Aries (sign of new beginnings, and individuality), suggest the birth of a new consciousness via higher superconscious perceptions (Uranus). There will be a much wider understanding of how we can shift our vibration and frequency, and co-create the future we want, with a quantum understanding of what we are doing. The whole process becomes conscious and empowering. This is one important way we can shift from some of the victim consciousness and dominance of old paradigm structures that have been evident in recent history.

All of us will be affected by these aspects, but there are certain groups of people who may resonate particularly strongly with Haumea in their birthchart. For instance, from 1953 to 1955, Haumea was conjunct Pluto in Leo. If you were born during those years, depending on other aspects in your chart, the combination of these planets could produce leadership for you particularly in areas of new consciousness and new thinking. You are likely to have a high degree of personal integrity too, and these qualities in you may become more prominent in the years leading up to 2020, and indeed beyond.

If you were born in 1962, you will have a Haumea-Uranus conjunction in your birthchart. Here, you are likely to have a more rebellious, radical, alternative view of the world, which is being stirred right now into a major awakening.

So the universe and recent planetary discoveries are supporting all that we have been outlining in this book, for your empowerment.

There will be enormous and fast-moving changes over the next three years, as there is an undeniable urge for economic, political, but also spiritual revolution. The consciousness of many people will shift, as abilities such as channelling, telepathy and healing will become commonplace. Most importantly, as we better understand the quantum nature of reality, we will take more responsibility for creating our own reality, whatever is happening in the outside world. We are each responsible for our own state of mind and being, and if we don't like the rapid change in the outer world we can decide to create a better reality. We are masters of our destiny. We each have the ability to create something magnificent in the world, and for ourselves.

Although we may go through some turbulence with the dismantling of the old paradigm to eventually fully move to the new paradigm, it has a tremendous feeling of excitement and empowerment, as we better understand how each of us plays a unique part in co-creating this world, and how we can use our own thinking and emotional shifts to create our own reality. It is well established now that our brains are neuroplastic and capable of great changes, but we will also increasingly understand how 'plastic' and flexible our reality is too. Start to see outer things and circumstances as less fixed, but merely the result of past thinking. That goes for your health too. Everything in your life is an extension of your energy expression from the past.

It is likely that with this shift in consciousness we will become aware of many more faculties that we can't even imagine at the moment. We will become much more empowered as individuals, and as humans. Abilities that have lain dormant will come to the fore, and we will develop much greater sensitivity to energy, understanding that it is what we, and the world, are made of.

There will be greater widespread understanding of how reality is formed in the quantum field, and how empowered we can be once we better understand our role as co-creators. The readers of this book have a significant advantage in this. Just think of the 'observer effect'; we are co-creating our own reality every second, mostly by default, until we become conscious of this process. We are also contributing to the global field of energy, so each of us is playing a part in how the world is unfolding. We can actually change our collective future, by acting together with peace and love. We are co-creators in every moment, so individually and together we are all shaping our future as we move towards 2020 and beyond.

Astrology can help us enormously to understand what our purpose is in this life. Through our focus on our North Node sign and house, and with that vision to guide us, we can have a life full of meaning, significance and individual contribution, whatever is happening in the tangible 3D world. That's what this book has been about.

So who will you be in this new world, and new paradigm? Can you envisage a role which resonates deeply with you, that continues your soul theme from many lifetimes, but has spiralled upwards in a new, powerful level of expression? How are you helping the world? What is your unique contribution? Do you feel now that you are operating from a deep, solid centre of self-knowing? One of the greatest gifts of astrology is self-understanding, but it goes beyond that, to become a language of our spiritual development. It is not static. In fact, the more you can work with your birthchart, the more you can express higher and higher levels of your potential. What you have learned in this book will help you enormously with navigating this paradigm shift. There are no limits, other than those we impose on ourselves.

Remember to find a spiritual anchor and centre in yourself that becomes your default position. This is where you live from. When challenged or stressed, have a fast mechanism to get you to that place. Whether that is through heart breathing, mindfulness, or whatever technique is best for you, know that you can change how your reality is unfolding if you observe events from that place of peace and love. Then that will be the frequency you are broadcasting, sending ripples of those emotions out to the world. Remember that as someone wisely said, whatever the question, love is the answer.

Afterword

"We know that man, essentially, is a being of light."

Fritz-Albert Popp

From all that you have learned in this book, you are now truly co-creating with the shifting patterns in the cosmos. You are no longer a victim of fate; you are empowered through this knowledge to create your own life much more consciously. You may even begin to stare up at the night sky in wonderment, recognising that you are made of stardust, and have direct connections in your life here on Earth to the constantly changing rhythms of the Moon. We live in a completely interconnected universe, and astrology is the secret language of interconnection. It inspires a sense of awe and magic in me.

You have come a very long way since you started reading this book. You now understand something that very few people do: the most secret part of this most secret language of astrology, your soul's purpose in this life, and in the context of many lifetimes. That is something profound, a gift for you.

Astrology is not only a language of interconnectedness, in that it is dealing at the same time with the outer heavenly movements and your inner psyche, but it is also a language of spiritual evolution. It helps us become aware of who we truly are, and what each of us is about in our lives this time around. It helps us to see that each of us is a divine, unique spark, in this vast tapestry of divine intelligence that weaves across time and space, and how each of us has a special role in the constant co-creation of our universe.

Blessings on your journey.

Bibliography and Recommended Reading

Astrology

Arroyo, Stephen, *Astrology, Psychology and the Four Elements; Astrology Karma and Transformation; Person-to-Person Astrology; Relationships and Life Cycles*

Baigent, Michael; Campion, Nicholas and Harvey, Charles, *Mundane Astrology*

Campion, Nicholas *A History of Western Astrology, Volumes I and II; The Book of World Horoscopes*

Evans, Jane A, *Twelve Doors to the Soul*

Elwell, Dennis, *The Cosmic Loom*

Gauquelin, Michel, *Written in the Stars*

Greene, Liz, *Saturn: A New Look at an Old Devil*

Hamblin, David, *Harmonic Charts*

Hand, Robert, *Planets in Transit*

Harding, Michael, *Hymns to the Ancient Gods*

Harding, Michael and Harvey, Charles, *Working with Astrology*

Harvey, Charles, *Anima Mundi*

Idemon, Richard, *The Magic Thread*

Merriman, Raymond, Forecast Books 2012 and 2013

Rudhyar, Dane, *Astrology of Personality*

Ruperti, Alexander, *Cycles of Becoming*

Sasportas, Howard, *The Twelve Houses; The Gods of Change*

Tompkins, Sue, *Aspects in Astrology; The Contemporary Astrologer's Handbook*

Tyl, Noel, *The Creative Astrology; Solar Arcs, Synthesis and Counselling;Vocations*

Quantum Physics, Science and Philosophy

Arntz, William; Chasse, Betsy and Vicente, Mark, *What the Bleep Do We Know!?*

Bohm, David, *The Essential David Bohm* (edited by Lee Nichol), *Unfolding Meaning; Wholeness and the Implicate Order*

Bohm, David and Krishnamurti, J, *The Ending of Time*

Bohm, David and Hiley, B J, *The Undivided Universe*

Chopra, Deepak, *SynchroDestiny*

Clark, Ronald W, *Einstein: The Life and Times*

Davies, Paul, *Superforce; The Cosmic Blueprint*

Dispenza, Dr Joe, *Evolve Your Brain; Break the Habit of Being Yourself*

Friedman, Norman, *Bridging Science and Spirit*

Herbert, Nick, *Quantum Reality*

László, Ervin, *Science and the Akashic Field*

Lipton, Bruce H, *Biology of Belief*

Martineau, John, *A Little Book of Coincidence in the Solar System*

McTaggart, Lynne, *The Intention Experiment*

Ober, Clinton; Sinatra, Stephen T; Zucker, Martin, *Earthing*

Pert, Candace B, *Molecules of Emotion*

Sheldrake, Dr Rupert, *A New Science of Life; The Rebirth of Nature*

Talbot, Michael, *Beyond the Quantum, Mysticism and the New Physics; The Holographic Universe*

Wilber, Ken, *Quantum Questions; The Holographic Paradigm*

Organisations Teaching Astrology

American Federation of Astrologers – www.astrologers.com
Centre for Psychological Astrology, London, UK – www.cpalondon.com
Faculty of Astrological Studies, London, UK – www.astrology.org.uk
London School of Astrology – www.londonschoolofastrology.co.uk
Mayo School of Astrology, London, UK – www.mayoastrology.com.
The Sophia Centre at Bath Spa University, UK – www.uwtsd.ac.uk/sophia
Noel Tyl, US – www.noeltyl.com
Federation of Australian Astrologers Inc. – www.faainc.org.au

Endnotes

1   HeartMath Global Coherence Initiative Website

2   HeartMath Global Coherence Initiative Website

3   Lynne McTaggart, *The Intention Experiment*, Free Press, New York, ISBN 0743276957, p104

4   Lynne McTaggart, *The Intention Experiment*, Free Press, New York, ISBN 0743276957, p110

5   Dean Radin, YouTube, 'The Global Consciousness Project'

6   Lynne McTaggart, *The Intention Experiment*, Free Press, New York, ISBN 0743276957

7   www.worldpeacegroup.org/washington_crime_study.html

8   www.greenmedinfo.com

9   Fred Alan Wolf in *The Quest for Wholeness: Healing Ourselves, Healing Our World*, by Robert Brumet

10 Tom Campbell, Conversation with Bruce Lipton on YouTube, 'Two Scientists See the Same World'

11 Dane Rudhyar, *The Astrology of Personality*, Chapter 9 (Santa Fe: Aurora 1991)

12 Dane Rudhyar, *The Astrology of Personality*, Chapter 9 (Santa Fe: Aurora 1991)

CPSIA information can be obtained
at www.ICGtesting.com
Printed in the USA
BVHW080304200821
614531BV00003B/303

9 781781 326848